BORDER OPTICS

CRITICAL CULTURAL COMMUNICATION

General Editors: Jonathan Gray, Aswin Punathambekar, Adrienne Shaw

Founding Editors: Sarah Banet-Weiser and Kent A. Ono

Border Optics

Surveillance Cultures on
the US-Mexico Frontier

Camilla Fojas

NEW YORK UNIVERSITY PRESS
New York

NEW YORK UNIVERSITY PRESS
New York
www.nyupress.org

References to Internet websites (URLs) were accurate at the time of writing. Neither the author nor New York University Press is responsible for URLs that may have expired or changed since the manuscript was prepared.

Cataloging-in-Publication data is available from the publisher.

Library of Congress Cataloging-in-Publication Data
Names: Fojas, Camilla, 1971–   author.
Title: Border optics : surveillance cultures on the US-Mexico frontier / Camilla Fojas.
Description: New York : New York University Press, [2021] | Series: Critical cultural communication | Includes bibliographical references and index.
Identifiers: LCCN 2020055450 | ISBN 9781479806980 (hardback) | ISBN 9781479807017 (paperback) | ISBN 9781479807055 (ebook) | ISBN 9781479807062 (ebook)
Subjects: LCSH: Border security—Social aspects—Mexican-American Border Region. | Border patrols—Social aspects—Mexican-American Border Region. | Video surveillance—Social aspects—Mexican-American Border Region. | United States—Boundaries—Mexico. | Mexico—Boundaries—United States.
Classification: LCC JV6565 .F65 2021 | DDC 363.28/509721—dc23
LC record available at https://lccn.loc.gov/2020055450

New York University Press books are printed on acid-free paper, and their binding materials are chosen for strength and durability. We strive to use environmentally responsible suppliers and materials to the greatest extent possible in publishing our books.

Manufactured in the United States of America

10 9 8 7 6 5 4 3 2 1

Also available as an ebook

CONTENTS

AUTHOR'S NOTE

This book was completed as the 2019 global pandemic was approaching a dark zenith and borders the world over were closed, including the southern and northern territorial borders of the United States and other US ports of entry, through imposed limits to international air travel. This exceptional state of affairs seemed to justify inflammatory nativist rhetoric about closing borders to protect the health and well-being of the nation. It also revealed profound social and economic divisions, further deepened by the economic shutdown and sealed borders. In response to the pandemic, the US government suspended surveillance at borders, technologies for sorting permissible entry from detention and deportation, and replaced it with barred entry. Crisis became an alibi for ever more restrictive immigration and asylum policies. Migrants and refugees petitioning at US borders were trapped in legal limbo, and those confined to detention centers were abandoned to exposure to the COVID-19 virus. The injustices at the border are not limited to times of crisis; they are only deepened by them. The outcome of the pandemic urges a renewed call to end the criminalization of migration, migrant detention and deportation, and targeting of racialized communities and to abolish the imperial border regime and its carceral complex.

Charlottesville, Virginia

Introduction

Border Óptica, or Seeing like a State

A career with borders but no boundaries.
—advertising copy to recruit Border Patrol agents

On an eerily moonless night in mid-November 2017, two Customs and Border Protection agents were tragically injured while patrolling the border in West Texas. Nobody knows precisely what happened, least of all the men involved. Rogelio Martinez succumbed to a massive head injury, while his partner, Stephen Garland, who sustained a concussion, survived without memory of the events of that night. The news media described this incident as a "mystery" and generated speculation about the possibility that these men endured a brutal assault by marauding migrants. According to the president of the National Border Patrol Council, Brandon Judd, "it was a grisly scene" around Martinez, and "his injuries were extensive," indicating that he was attacked from behind and "struck in the head with rocks, or multiple rocks."[1] Judd's comment deepens the intrigue around the specter of an unseen and dangerous force, defiant of borders and their legal bounds.

In February 2018, the Federal Bureau of Investigation (FBI) ruled Agent Martinez's death an accident. According to the FBI report, he ran off the edge of the road in the dark of night into an unfenced culvert, followed directly by Garland. This account diverges from that of the president of the National Border Patrol Council, yet each interpretation lends a similar valence to the figure of the migrant as an abstract menace. In the FBI's conclusion, the Border Patrol agents in pursuit of a mobile threat are driven into the dark chasm of the borderlands in a manner consonant with the earliest story lines of both Hollywood and Mexican cultural productions that associate the border with the unknown as a site of incipient violence in the conflict between warring

1

races and nations. Or, as Judd insinuates, the migrants lay waste to the law with primitive tools and atavistic techniques, leveraging their position through the surprise attack, triggering outrage over other similar assaults perpetrated by unknown or unforeseen assailants threatening national sovereignty and security, from the alleged strike on the battleship USS *Maine* in Havana Harbor and the bombing of Pearl Harbor to the events of September 11, 2001. This moment reveals the ideological imaginary of the border optic from the Global North in which migrants enact violence on agents of the state. Yet the history of the borderlands is not one of an injured state but of genocide, of migrants' death by US policy and institutions and ongoing White-supremacist vigilante and Border Patrol and police violence.

The border agents' experience evokes the mythos of the border as a shadowy abyss of meaning and a significant social and cultural divide. These events seem like the plot of a movie; they could be drawn from a fictional story line about the mistaken identities and mystifying motives of borderland denizens caught up in international intrigue, reminiscent of *Touch of Evil* (1958). Like Orson Welles's dark saga, the scenario is pure border noir, with its preoccupation with vision and sight, about what can be seen and the obscurities and ambiguities of the imagination. The fantasmatic spectacle of the Border Patrol under ambush emblematizes a state of injury ensuing from a surprise attack, the threat that justifies the logic of preemption. Haunting this scene is the migrant as a ghostly apparition, an invisible force discursively produced along intersecting gendered and racialized lines that trace the contours of the mythic Mexican bandit. The entire media melodrama signals the failures of the security state, in which the surveillant apparatus is off track, unseeing, misguided and misguiding, generating its own self-destruction. The migrant, imagined as a mobile and marauding agent, is the horizon of interpretation of the security apparatus at the border and the key hermeneutic figure of the violent state project of *borderveillance*, or the culture, politics, and infrastructure of border surveillance; the latter is the apex of a global security regime underwritten by a corporate-military alliance and based in colonial histories of racial capitalism, a system of capital accumulation accomplished through the production of racial inequity.

This book explores border optics as a visual archive and the optical infrastructure of the US-Mexico borderlands that, together, constitute the cultural technologies of borderveillance, charged with the force of imperial affect. The optics of the border have various interwoven layers of meanings and modes, from the imaginary to the material: from the popular mediations of the borderlands dating back to the nineteenth-century border-security and immigration policies to the security infrastructure at the border, what Lisa Parks describes as the "stuff you can kick," stuff that nonetheless harbors its own symbolic tributaries of meaning.[2] Borderveillance marks the integration of these structures of signification and material effects. It is a way of seeing and surveying that is freighted with national security concerns and colonial histories in which seeing is sorting and migrants are visually apprehended as a prelude to arrest and detention. The US-Mexico border is an archeologically layered visual space of policing within a technological matrix, one that is seen from watchtowers, camera-mounted vehicles, helicopters, surveillance balloons, tethered aerostat radar systems (TARS), unmanned aerial vehicles (UAVs), live-streaming websites, and ground-level tracking, and one that is visualized across various cultural forms and genres of media, from newsreel reenactments of border skirmishes during the Mexican Revolution, painting, photography, border film and television, social media, border-security technologies, borderland maps, architectural models, Homeland Security strategic plans, congressional reports, and news media.

Borders are the subject of an expanding market of cultural productions, surveillance products, and technologies supported by an imbricated government and corporate security apparatus. *Border Optics* examines these cultures of border security as part of a deeply historical visual regime and surveillant infrastructure—while the security infrastructure also captures nonvisual sensory data, for example, through heat sensing, radio-wave detection, directional listening devices, or ground sensing, all data are shaped by the hegemony of the visible. Nonvisual data-apprehension technologies serve as support or precursors to visual and actual apprehension within a representationally encoded register. Seeing from the perspective of the border presupposes a division of apprehension; it means discerning between those who are deserving of the entitlements of belonging and those who are not. The visual codes of border control are premised on a truth regime that delineates the proper, legible, legal, and assimilable migrant from

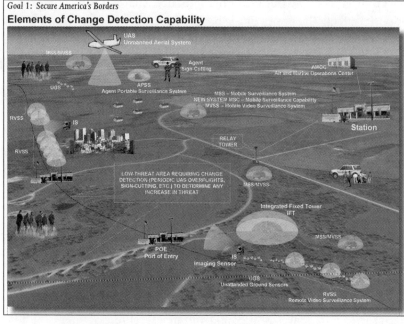

Figure 1.1. Diagram of total surveillance from the 2012 Customs and Border Protection strategic plan. (US Customs and Border Protection, *2012–2016 Border Patrol Strategic Plan*, 12)

the unassimilable, inscrutable, extralegal alien. The primary aim of this complex of industry, state, and private endeavors is not simply enforcement but control, particularly of the movement of goods and people in accordance with the split codes of the border-security imaginary. Any resistant or oppositional politics must contend with this deeply entrenched colonial and racial capitalist imaginary.

Border Optics does not endeavor to provide an exhaustive account of the visual archive and surveillant apparatus of the US-Mexico borderlands. Instead, it explores several related cultural media and apparatuses that have shaped a dominant way of seeing, energized by the affective force of the history of the region. This includes a countervision apparent in revisionist border historical accounts, art, media, architectural design, and activist movements, along with the strains of subversion within the dominant view. This book explores the resistance inherent in elucidating the failures, fissures, and vulnerabilities in the surveillant regime, ones

account

that migrants expose in their enterprising, insurrectionary, and creative routes over, under, and through national limits. Thus, this is not an account of control on the one hand and resistance on the other but of an imbrication and complicated matrix of these forces. However, the disruption of the illusion of total state control has powerful political implications. Each chapter of *Border Optics* explores the border optic along different surveillant axes, from the ambitious Department of Homeland Security plan for an integrated border surveillance network, or the Secure Border Initiative (SBI), serialized television docuseries about border security, the Texas Virtual Border Watch Program, the cultural and technological instances of border drone surveillance and countersurveillance, and nature television docuseries and documentaries about the ecological consequences of border security to the international border-security corporate-state alliance and adaptation of surveillant technologies that seek to globalize and automate border security for the expansion of racial surveillance capitalism.

Optical Illusions

Border Optics draws on the currency that "optics" has in public discourse and institutional settings as a way of indicating control over perception, how something appears, with emphasis on the apprehending role of the viewing public. Along US borders, it means managing the "optics" of border security. As Peter Andreas notes, "'successful' border management depends on successful image management," and "the escalation of border policing has been less about deterring than about image crafting."[3] Andreas, writing in the late 1990s, post-NAFTA (North American Free Trade Agreement) era, explores the image management of the region as part of an effort to project control as the liberalization of trade seemed to suggest the opposite: the loss of control of national borders. The immigration regime generates the spectacle of migrant illegality and projects it onto the border region, creating a demand for what Nicholas De Genova calls a "spectacle of enforcement."[4] Jonathan Inda notes that mass media of the era collapses the "out of control" border with unchecked immigration for which enhanced policing is the only remedy, a scenario that set the stage for the massive expansion of the border surveillance apparatus and enforced deviation from urban to dangerous desert routes of transit.[5] This inaugurated an unprecedented era of migrant death by the weaponized borderlands, a region that Jason De León excavates as the land of open graves, a sinister permutation of the meaning of "open" as it is attributed to the post-NAFTA borderlands.[6] Indeed, the association of free trade with open borders, ubiquitous at the time, is prevalent across many popular films and TV shows. In *Traffic* (2000), a narco-trafficker opines that NAFTA enables his work, while a similar line of reasoning circulates in other media, including *A Man Apart* (2003) and the TV series *Kingpin* (NBC, 2003)—all of which convey the targets of border policing, migrants and drugs, while associating the increase in traffic in contraband and migrant mobility with porous borders.[7] Andreas notes that border policing in the late 1990s is more often a performance for public consumption. He notes that the image of the border glosses the policy contradictions that arise with free trade: "The simultaneous creation of a borderless economy and a barricaded border may seem paradoxical and has certainly created some awkward policy tensions and dilemmas. Yet as I have stressed, part of the political project of turning the border into a more expansive economic bridge has also involved making it at least appear to be a more formidable police barrier."[8] The border drama and its optical display and infrastructure in a post-9/11 world are concerned with the appearance of a "security environment" framed by surveillance technologies that extract profit from migrant circulation while anticipating future threats.[9] This post-9/11 security environment requires engaging different objectives, ones oriented toward threats unknown, not simply migrants and drugs but the surprise attack, the caravan, the sanctuary movement, and other forms of unpredictable migrant mobility, resistance, and insurrection.

By 1993, US immigration policy shifted toward controlling "unwanted immigration" with the "prevention through deterrence" program or "Operation Blockade" in El Paso, which coincided with a rise in public concern over the social burden of undocumented migration and fears about migrants as a criminal class.[10] This public sentiment crescendoed in 2006, the year that marks the culmination of policies linking immigration to criminality, what the legal scholar Juliet Stumpf calls "crimmigration," drawing from a 2006 *Washington Post* article describing immigration detention camps as "crimmigration camps," where undocumented migrants are incarcerated without due process and treated as criminals. Stumpf notes the splitting of this political imaginary in a manner that reflects the discriminatory practice of social sorting: "The changes in the law fed a powerful vision of the immigrant as a scofflaw and a criminal that began to dominate the competing image of the benign, hard-working embodiment of the American dream."[11] This image of the migrant shadowed by criminality and suspicion inflected subsequent mediations across cultural productions and security regimes and ultimately became the basis of a hegemonic border optic.

The idea that all migrants seeking entry at the southern territorial border of the United States are "undesirable crimmigrants" is an effect of social sorting and an outcome of this arbitrary and historically shifting geographical boundary. Oscar Gandy describes this manner of differentiation as the "panoptic sort" to show how database marketing sorts consumers according to their value to companies.[12] David Lyon applies this logic to other domains to show how the differential application of surveillance techniques underscores a hierarchical social order that discriminates between groups "to sort and sift populations, to categorize and to classify, to enhance the life chances of some and to retard those of others."[13] For Elia Zureik and Mark Salter, this sifting of groups is an effect of borders and boundaries. They define surveillance in terms of the social sorting commissioned by borders. Moreover, the policing of mobility through the techniques and technologies of surveillance serve border and boundary maintenance, sustaining divisions and exclusions.[14] Surveillance cultures generate borders of various kinds. By the same token, surveillant techniques might undo or unsettle borders, move and rearrange them, shift their meanings and reorganize power relations, thereby enabling revisions to the border optic to prefigure a debordered and decolonial future.[15] In this way, the border is a way of seeing, an "epistemic angle," that for Sandro Mezzadra and Brett Neilson is also "method" or manner and object of research, a site of transformation of political power and sovereignty along the axes and flows of capital and labor migration.[16]

Another tributary of the meaning of optics distributes the capacity for visual apprehension to other animacies and media, from animals to machines. The optics of the camera or the mediations and enhancements of the visual rendered by various data-capture technologies, from camera-mounted drones or UAVs and night-vision scopes to automatic facial, iris, gait, voice, and fingerprint recognition, point to the separation and enhancement of vision from human capacities and limitations. It is also the optics of underground and undersea fiber-optic cabling, particularly in the proposal that such technologies substitute physical barriers along the border, enabling the widening of the technical net of apprehension. The border optic refers to the expanded vision of the border as a consequence of the interface of militarism, technology, and the media archive of the region, which all work inextricably together. The border is both laboratory and archive, indexing an optical regime and a way of seeing drawn from maps, geographical and geological surveys, military strategic plans, paintings, illustrations, photographs, postcards, novels, film, and television—all of which combine fascination with the region with the visual codes of surveillance and survey.

Optics signals a complete visual apparatus, from recording and representation to the infrastructure and institutions that support the visual regime. For Friedrich Kittler, "optical media" is a systematic integration of storage, transmission, and processing that finds a perfect instantiation in the "medium of all media," the computer.[17] The computer supersedes all previous media forms, accedes to autonomy, and marks the final rupture from technological dependency on the human body. It is the culmination of optical media that derives from the military and the instrumental use of media for strategic defense purposes. While Kittler writes loosely of the historical and cultural context of this origin story, his analysis works well in domains where militarism shapes public discourse, particularly for contested and secured borders.[18] In these contexts, the computer, in its integrated functionality, allegorizes the desire of the military for total future coordination and control across the various regimes and institutions of local, national, and global security.

David Burnham, writing before Kittler and on the cusp of the year made symbolic by George Orwell, in 1983, signals a warning about the "computer state," one that gathers and filters information for the concentration of technocratic power. Technocratic institutions manage information for the purpose of surveillance and social control. In the computer state, the National Security Agency is the "ultimate computer bureaucracy."[19] Burnham's warning about the erosion of democratic process by the computer was ominously prescient. Decades later, after

9/11, control is preemptive and predictive, not responsive to available or known threats but to opaque and unanticipated ones. The manner and level of coordination and control imagined by Burnham remains a speculative fantasy, one that sustains and supports the mythos of the infallibility and determinacy of technology and the inevitability of a technocratic future.

Kelly Gates, Shoshana Magnet, and other critics of the technological future heralded by biometric control resist the force and ideology of technocratic inevitability. Magnet explores the failures of surveillance technologies, specifically biometrics, as a consequence of structural failures based in systemic inequities. For example, she describes how "smart borders," or the use of automated border controls along US-Canadian ports of entry, are not neutral but are deployed to justify the targeting of some migrants to enable smooth entry for business travelers; moreover, they sort travelers using xenophobic tropes and racialized criteria.[20] Gates notes that the mandatory use of biometric technology in the mid-1990s for border crossing cards (BCCs), designed to enable short-term travel from Mexico, targets and tracks—via biographical data, facial image, digital fingerprints, and a control number—Mexican border crossers, whereas a similar program for business travelers remained voluntary.[21] The automated fingerprint-based biometric tracking system IDENT, first deployed in the San Diego sector of Border Patrol, is used to track repeat border crossers in search of criminal offenders.[22] In this split bordering logic, efficiency for privileged travelers means intensified targeting for "unwanted" migrants.

Borderveillance is a combination of vigilance and visual sorting underwritten by a vast political economy of surveillance, one with a long history in colonial practices of social control that expanded at an unprecedented rate during the rise of the "War on Terror." The United States workshopped surveillance techniques in the Philippines after the Spanish-American War and gradually developed them further in wars in the Middle East, in Iraq and Afghanistan, adding new technologies to these procedures to eventually bring them back to the US-Mexico border, notably in the form of camera-mounted Predator drones and surveillance balloons.[23] These technologies are symptoms of borderveillance as a form of power within an optical regime that would render its subjects permanently visible. Caren Kaplan, whose musings on aerial views begin with the aftermath of the "War on Terror," notes that visual control operates from above and that, while aerial power is a function of war, it expands to consolidate and enforce colonial power more generally.[24] This aerial power signals greater war power in what Eyal Weizman calls the "politics of verticality."[25] For Peter Adey, the view from the sky, exemplified by the airplane, changes the experience of space along the axes of perspective and scale. The aerial view implies and is moored to the ground-level view; rather than separate, they are mutually constitutive and reside together in "vertical reciprocity."[26] The border optic is multiperspectival and operates within and beyond the vertical dynamic of above and below. It is a view from above, at ground level, while it also operates below ground and below sea level. Security and surveillance at the border concerns, in equal measure, scenarios that take place on the ground and below it as well as at and under sea. The tunnel and tunneling, submarine passage, and other forms of taking cover and concealment are part of the repertoire of creative moves from the Global South that allow moving bodies to escape unnoticed and unseen from the aerial vantage of imperial power. This defiance of visual apprehension disrupts the illusion of state control of the field of the visible.

Border Optics explores a vital aspect of the rise of the surveillance state through the expansion of border control and surveillance with a focus on the paradigmatic border between the Global North and the Global South, the US-Mexico border, as both an archeologically layered geopolitical space and a highly mediated visual field. US borders, from the contested southern border to their expansion into the Caribbean and the Pacific, constitute the front lines of US border imperialism as sites where imperial chauvinism is projected and disseminated. For the writer-activist Harsha Walia, border imperialism is an outcome of the intersecting logics of security and racial capitalism, evinced in the commission of international boundaries and the production of borders of various kinds, including the enclosure of the commons and racial, gender, and labor stratifications. Walia delineates border imperialism into four "overlapping and concurrent structurings" that show how the border is the nexus of oppression: "First, the mass displacement of impoverished and colonized communities resulting from asymmetrical relations of global power, and the simultaneous securitization of the border against those migrants whom capitalism and empire have displaced;

second, the criminalization of migration with severe punishment and discipline of those deemed 'alien' or 'illegal'; third, the entrenchment of a racialized hierarchy of citizenship by arbitrating who legitimately constitutes the nation-state; and fourth, the state-mediated exploitation of migrant labor, akin to conditions of slavery and servitude, by capital interests."[27] "Border imperialism" refers to modes of governance in which the bounded nation, defined by its exclusions, operates in conjunction with the dictates of global capitalism. Each nation polices its borders to ensure smooth flows of global capital within and beyond it, while controlling the mobility of migrants. In the United States, border control is a function of imperial overreach, and its historical and geopolitical dimensions are indexed to the southern borderlands as a contested colonial space and a site for the projection of US power.

The history of the borderlands is a history of efforts to wrest control of the region as a sign of effective national dominion. Oscar Martínez describes the region as a zone of trouble and site of local resistance and challenge to centralized authority.[28] Surveillance of the US-Mexico border is a function of broader militarization of the region and a consequence of imperial efforts to domesticate and incorporate ceded Mexican territories into the US national project. Those borderland territories, annexed to the United States as a result of the Treaty of Guadalupe Hidalgo and other efforts to cede Mexican land, constituted over half of the total area of the Republic of Mexico. The revised national demarcations of this geopolitical space do not alter its cultural contours, which remain unchanged and delineated by its peoples, described by Américo Paredes as "Greater Mexico." For Paredes, "Greater Mexico" has a broad cultural register that includes "all the areas inhabited by people of Mexican culture—not only within the present limits of the Republic of Mexico but in the United States as well—in a cultural rather than political sense."[29] José Limón explores the affective register of this internal alterity. For Limón, "Greater Mexico" refers to "all Mexicans, beyond Laredo and from either side" of the border, a zone shaped by the discourse of White supremacy and the ambivalences and contradictions of highly cathected racialized encounters and intimacies.[30] Alan Eladio Gómez highlights the political dimension of the term, in which "Greater Mexico" is a postnational political imaginary that recalls a history of struggle and resistance in the Global South while it points to a revolutionary future.[31] Alicia Schmidt

Camacho shows how transborder solidarity impacts the political conditions of migrants through the recognition of their historical embeddedness in the borderlands.[32] The persistence of a common culture and the potential for transborder political alliance and activism ignites US defensive guarding of these territories against the idea of *Aztlán*, the restoration of the legendary homeland of the Aztecs.

The border and borderlands are jealously guarded against separation through the ongoing habits of imperial chauvinism. Prior to annexation, the US government regarded territories of Mexico with a covetous gaze—one of the earliest sites of interest was Texas, where Anglo-Americans fled and settled to escape taxation. US attempts to purchase Texas in 1826 and 1830 were rebuffed by Mexico. The desire to buy Texas transformed into coercive rage that found expression in increasingly aggressive foreign policy, initiating what Rodolfo Acuña describes as a "legacy of hate."[33] In 1834, the first US governor of Mexican Texas, Henry Smith, published his screed *Security for Texas*, outlining measures necessary to secure the territory.[34] Smith is characterized by his biographer as one of the pioneers of Texas, but he might more accurately be described as a settler colonialist, or someone who occupies and commandeers land for private interest and with violent disregard for native inhabitants. The need for security and the fear that former pieces of Mexico might return to its original benefactor presaged a movement during the Mexican Revolution in the early 1900s of revolt against imperial Anglo tyranny. The Texas-Mexican "Plan de San Diego," signed by over one thousand people in San Diego, Texas, promulgated a break from "Yankee tyranny" through rebellion by a "Liberating Army for Races and Peoples" that would form an independent republic composed of Texas, New Mexico, Colorado, Arizona, and California—all lands taken from Mexico by the United States. It also called for the death of all Anglo males over the age of sixteen residing in this territory. The US response to this insurrection was devastating, with hundreds of Mexican Americans lynched and executed by Texas Rangers and vigilantes, leading to the expansion of Anglo control through violent repression.[35] This force of historical affect of jealous dispossession and anxious defense animates border policy and political discourses about the Southwest; it is but one of a panoply of affects deployed to justify intensified security at US frontiers.

The social anxiety about the erosion of Anglo supremacy, under-written by land tenure and guided by hispanophobia, has evolved into anticipation of a menacing "Latino threat," located and operative in the borderlands, as the affective work of national security cultures.[36] The border-security experts and scholars James Phelps, J. Michael Boze-man, and Monica Koenigsberg explore variations on fears about Latinx annexation of the Southwest as a prelude to complete hegemony. Phelps, Bozeman, and Koenigsberg engage in "private conversations" with Border Patrol agents about border-security culture, or how the latter, as petty sovereigns, enact the concepts of sovereignty and security.[37] They note that, unlike other secured border regions, the US-Mexico border-lands has a unique character and defining security optic around the vexed issue of occupation. That is, other regions are not haunted by both a past and a political ideal of deoccupation or the idea that the border region is merely occupied and is destined to be returned to its rightful provenance. The security experts consolidate, from their conversations with career border agents, an array of occupation-oriented conditions, principles, and assumptions basic to local border-security culture. These assumptions, subject to disabuse in the authors' estimation, include the idea that a Latinx majority signals political power and that the southwest-ern United States belongs to Mexico.[38] Ultimately, the authors argue for a realpolitik of border security premised on a typology of inclusion and exclusion that forms the basis of social sorting, or the uncritical quandary of "how to build barriers to keep out those not wanted, while allowing the maximum possible legal movement of people and commodities?"[39] It should be noted that border-security scholarship is part of a particular type of unreconstructed state-oriented security studies and is distinct not just from critical security studies but also from border studies scholarship that emerges at the intersection of various fields including postnational or postregional historical studies, trans-American studies, Latin Ameri-can studies, and critical race and ethnic studies; "critical" denotes a move to interrogate and revise official or canonical areas of inquiry and study.

Border-Security Nation

Border security, often deemed a regional issue, becomes, at times, a national obsession subsequent to immigration policy mood swings. By the early 2000s, the border found its way into small-town America with the expansion of the immigration-enforcement and migrant-detention infrastructure to the interior of the nation.[40] During the 2018 midterm elections, candidates in midwestern towns with little or no immigrant populations in their midst were caught up in debates about the effectiveness of border-security technologies. The imagined potential "invasion" of border-crossing migrants into the nation's interior is reflected in entertainment media, apparent in the show *Ozark* (Netflix, 2017–). A money launderer from Chicago migrates to the Ozarks, drawing his Mexican drug-trafficking associates deeper into the heartland. While Chicago is a major transit point for narcotics and drug-trade profits, the Ozarks are marginal to this world and a surprising node in its complex network that implicates the United States as a major consumer nation.

The expansion of border transit bolsters the widespread notion that we have what Howard Buffett, son of the investor and philanthropist Warren Buffett, calls "our 50-state border crisis" or what the activist and writer Todd Miller calls the "Border Patrol nation" in his eponymous book.[41] In 2014, US representative Jeff Duncan of South Carolina echoed a similar sentiment during a hearing about the Arizona Border Surveillance Technology Plan when he intoned, "Security at the southwest border is very important to folks in South Carolina and across this nation."[42] Likewise, the legal critic Anil Kalhan describes the "immigration surveillance state" as a regime of mass detention and deportation that, he argues, signals an approach to governance and state control that is no longer limited to border zones—apparent in the incorporation of Immigration and Customs Enforcement (ICE), responsible for interior apprehensions and removals, and Customs and Border Protection (CBP) to the Department of Homeland Security in 2002, a move that expanded the CBP's national-security mandate.

Moreover, the Securities Program empowers local law enforcement to act as border agents. Any revision to or reform of this system would simply reinforce and expand it. For example, the surveillance apparatus expanded with "earned legalization" through the Immigration Reform and Control Act of 1986, which granted permanent residence to migrants. Those who were granted green cards had to meet certain criteria and provide extensive documentation and submit to biometric and biographical information gathering.[43] They are subject to intensive surveillance even after meeting the eligibility requirements and must continue to provide documentation that proves they are conducting themselves in an exemplary manner, not just as law-abiding but in a manner consistent with social norms. The state retains the potential to vacate immigrants' rights to naturalization and citizenship—even after such matters have long been adjudicated, notable in the cases of contested birth certificates issued by midwives in border towns.[44] Legalization programs reinforce the surveillance state by producing documented legal immigrants as readily delegitimized aliens.

Border security includes the artifacts and objects of surveillance, while it is also a process and set of procedures. It is a performance, and ports of entry are its theatrical space. Each time a checkpoint or port of entry is traversed, travelers perform the same ritualized security practices, exposing their bodies and possessions to review and responding to similar questions about their person. Airport travelers must enact a choreographed performance of what Rachel Hall calls the "transparent traveler." As we perform our docility to surveillance through our willingness to be processed and probed, the symbolic power of state security is asserted. The border-security complex is political theater for the performance of control, a space of ritual that, through its mimetic dynamic, contains the kernel of resistance within it.[45] The price of entry is submission and absolute truth-telling, or the performance of the "aesthetics of transparency."[46] US border agents are in constant pursuit of deception, of the gap between the performance and the "truth" displayed by bodily expressions, which is particularly problematic for those whose gender marker on legal identification documents does not match the gender they present.[47] In the various procedural TV docuseries about the US-Mexico border and other ports of entry, the emphasis on veracity and authenticity exposes a deeply vexed truth regime, one that is troubled by the exceptional space of the border, in which due process is suspended.

US ports of entry are sites where due process is not simply suspended but inverted, where subjects are guilty or suspicious before proven innocent. Moreover, when we face security at ports of entry, particularly airports, we are subject to screenings that would, in any other context, be a violation of Fourth Amendment protections against warrantless searches and seizures. Along US borders, Customs and Border Protection agents, under the auspices of the Department of Homeland Security, are granted the right to perform warrantless searches on anyone deemed suspicious within one hundred miles of the US perimeter. The American Civil Liberties Union calls this the "constitution-free zone of the United States."[48] Todd Miller describes this zone as exemplary of similar force-fields of security in other spaces guarded by agents of CBP, such as Greyhound and Amtrak stations and vehicles and the various locations of the Super Bowl games.[49] These spaces function as pop-up security theaters, replete with the infrastructure, personnel, and technologies found at US ports of entry. Security screening is everywhere, or as Rapiscan Systems describes the function of its screening technology as it relates to people, "Once reserved for access to secure areas, people screening has become so commonplace it is now enforced not only at airports, government and corrections facilities but also at stadiums, movie theaters, cruise ships, and elsewhere."[50] The open-ended "elsewhere" registers ominously with the indeterminacy of ubiquity.

Punish by Proxy

The theater of security is bolstered and reflected in the actual theater of the border or the literal mediation and representation of this zone through the historical and ongoing production of images and story lines about borders. As mentioned earlier, in the United States, the prevailing history of the border is that of the US-Mexico border, conveyed across popular culture in dime-store westerns of the early nineteenth century to contemporary westerns, drug-trafficking media, border-security docuseries, and various other media about the border. These stories tend to present similar tropes and themes that accord with the mood swings of immigration policy, premised on the prevailing moral universe of each genre, typically of good guys against bad guys and story lines based on a chase in the pursuit of justice. The good guys are variously Texas Rangers, deputized cowboys, and the most enduring figure of borderlands justice, the Border Patrol agent. The latter is the most iconic figure of border media, outpacing its mythic predecessor of the Texas Ranger for its broader geographic scope and transmedia and transgenre popularity. The advent of the Border Patrol in 1924 formalized and technologized border surveillance, putting the Border Patrol agent on the front lines of national security.

Like the Texas Ranger, the Border Patrol agent has a long, mythic fictional and nonfictional cultural history. One of the earliest lionizing accounts of the Border Patrol is by Mary Kidder Rak, whose historical tale, published in 1938, illustrates the cardinal tropes of the border-surveillance apparatus. The book imaginatively renders policing activity at the border, while it is both celebration and exposé of the inner workings of the Border Patrol, which, as a relatively new policing institution, is the object of patriotically charged fascination. Rak asserts her fidelity to this organization on the dedication page, which reads, "To my friends in the United States Immigration and Naturalization Service," thus making clear the ideological vantage of the narration as one aligned with the state. The promotional copy on the book jacket underscores her unprecedented access to the organization:

> This is the dramatic story of the Watch-Dog of the Mexican Border. Mrs. Rak made friends with the officers of the border patrol and was given access to the files at the various headquarters in western Texas, New Mexico, and Arizona. The officers were modest, but the facts were there, and little by little she unearthed a series of exciting stories about the smuggling of aliens and narcotics across the line, about patrolling on both sides of the border and back into the mountains, about the enormous influx of Chinese during the depression, and about hundreds of thrilling adventures in the course of the day's work of the patrol.

Rak's account of the Border Patrol reveals the continual recurrence of the same tropes and topics, particularly in the "thrilling" excitement of tales of pursuit of migrants—mostly Mexican and Chinese workers—and the righteous moral affect elicited by stories of the law triumphing over smugglers of contraband. Moreover, the book introduces the border-surveillance imaginary as a visual regime that links security to immigration and is symbolically preemptive in the strategic deployment of punishment by proxy.

Mary Kidder Rak represents the vantage of a borderlands transplant capable of translating local experience into a national-security idiom. She was born in Iowa, lived for a time in San Francisco, and settled in the Arizona borderlands, where she and her husband each owned a cattle ranch that they merged into a single compound. Her book is often considered part of the historical record of the Border Patrol. Kelly Lytle Hernández, in her extensive history of this policing entity, describes Rak's work as more of an artifact of the intimacy of ranchers and farmers with Border Patrol agents during the 1930s. Ranchers were unofficially deputized agents who aided and supported the Border Patrol in the capture of migrants, both Mexican and Chinese, to signal their coordinated control of migrant mobility in the region and thereby exert dominion over the labor market. The inception of the Border Patrol marked the origin of the distinction between immigrants and migrant workers; Mexicans and Chinese were of the latter, that is, workers whose presence was deemed temporary and who were not expected to become immigrants.[51] During this era, the Border Patrol practiced selective enforcement of immigration laws, policing Mexican migrants seeking work, not to hinder their entry but to manage the flow of labor in obeisance to the needs of ranchers and farmers. In turn, the Border Patrol could call on ranchers like the Raks for aid when they needed supplemental surveillance.[52] Rak's historical document records the origin of the human resources and technologies, the nascent infrastructure, of border surveillance.

The first image of Rak's *Border Patrol*, facing the title page, is that of a "steel watch tower," described as "complete with a 'crow's nest,'" in which the observer has "a comprehensive view of both banks of the Rio Grande." This single image indexes the modern form of policing at the border as surveillance and presages its technological future, the fixed integrated tower equipped with cameras and radar. The opening anecdote about border security begins with the decline of the Texas Rangers' mythic dominion and the rise of a modern policing organization and form of governmentality that marks a shift from the spectacle of punishment to the infrastructure of surveillance, of which the watch tower is a symbol. Rak conveys this early logic of punishment by proxy through anecdote. She writes of a town distraught by unruly marauding Mexicans who deputize a retired Texas Ranger, who is "given a free hand" to restore law to the town.

Many early Border Patrol agents were former Rangers. The Texas Rangers, originally a protopolicing force deployed to restore law and order, are the origin of vigilante lawlessness in the United States, in which the "ends justify the means" or, in this case, "no one was to question his methods if he produced the desired results."⁵³ This story infuses the Border Patrol with the Texas Ranger mythos. Like the men outnumbered at the Alamo, but this time by design, the Ranger in Rak's story declines the help of a force of men and chooses only a single man, "a cowboy, who had come from a distance and was unhampered by local ties."⁵⁴ He is a "lone Ranger" and part of the legend that suggests a single Ranger could quell a mass riot, thus the saying "one Ranger, one riot." He would use the power of spectacle to subjugate his targets, along with the Texas Ranger practice of punishment or "revenge by proxy." He and his cowboy sidekick round up Mexicans weakened by drink and chain them to a "great length of heavy log," until "the whole length of log chain was alive with angry, bewildered, and frightened men." Those who evade capture and flee bring back stories to Mexico of the "strange and terrifying performances of 'one old man with white hair and a fat young one.'"⁵⁵ The tales of this spectacle are broadcast widely across the border, and some of the men are released with the purpose of conveying the message that all property stolen from the United States must be restored to the northern bank of the river in order to exact the release of the imprisoned men.

Border control is a spectacle of violence for the purpose of the protection and defense of private property, to which bodies of Mexicans are collateralized by proxy. "Before night fell there were 'returns from outlying districts.' Horses, cows, plows, hens, tools, wagons, everything that could be carried or driven across a stream came back to the northern bank of the Rio Grande; for sons, brothers, and husbands were locked to that diabolical log chain, and mothers, sisters, and wives feared the worst if stolen property was not speedily returned. At the end of twenty-four hours the hostages were released and jubilant Americans went down to the riverbank to reclaim their goods and chattels."⁵⁶ This story becomes a mythic reminder of the arbitrary power of the United States and of strategies and methods of punishment that, as Rak intones, are no longer necessary because of the "hard, persistent, and successful work of the Border Patrol."⁵⁷ In fact, Border Patrol strategies merely shifted from symbolic detention to rendering the borderlands a permanent field of the visible, where all Mexicans are under suspicion, not just a totemic few. Rak transfers the legacy of the Texas Rangers to the Border Patrol agents, who inherit the mythic proportions but not, ostensibly, the extralegal practices of their predecessors.

This association recalls the work of the renowned historian of the Texas Rangers, Walter Prescott Webb, who published the definitive tome *The Texas Rangers* just three years prior to Rak's *Border Patrol*. Just as Webb documents the closing of the frontier and the waning of the Texas Rangers' preeminence, Rak writes of the Border Patrol agents maintaining the order restored and protected by their predecessors. The Rangers were few in number, animating the tale of the lone lawman, and Border Patrol agents are likewise framed as small in number from their very origins, "a handful of men," in what will become a constant refrain of US public discourse about the limited or lacking resources, human and technological, for border security.

Rak's story of the spectacle of punishment nicely allegorizes the interwoven theater and practice of border security, in which the symbolic threat of consequence is a key part of the story of US border patrol. In this history, the bodies of Mexican migrants are held both as proxies for criminals and as collateral for the debts incurred by criminal expropriation. This continual collapse of signification, the elision of Mexican and criminal, in the use of proxies shapes the ongoing legacy of border patrol in the Southwest. This was a common Texas Ranger practice, mentioned earlier, of "revenge by proxy," that, along with "one ranger, one riot" and "shoot now, ask questions later," was a core dictum of the Ranger mythos. Monica Muñoz Martinez excavates and eloquently documents the history of anti-Mexican violence in Texas and the legacies of the state of terror created by the Texas Rangers. Law enforcement would enact, collude in, and aid in covering up violence against Mexicans, from assault to lynching, to maintain White dominance in political and economic institutions along the border. This state-sanctioned violence is at the very foundation and origin of the state.[58]

In Américo Paredes's demythologizing account, he summarizes Texas Ranger legend and writes of how the Texas Rangers put "the Texan's pseudo folklore into deeds."[59] Among the many racist and prejudicial ideas animating Ranger protocol was the notion that "the Mexican is cruel by nature" and must be met with preemptively cruel treatment. Moreover, Mexicans, according to legend, are treacherous and prone to thievery. Their mestizo, or mixed-race, nature makes them degenerate and debauched. And finally, the master mytheme is embodied in the Ranger: "The Texan has no equal anywhere, but within Texas itself there developed a special breed of men, The Texas Rangers, in whom the Texan's qualities reached their culmination."[60] This legend is not simply the stuff of folklore and oral tradition but of mainstream print media, from newspapers to scholarly texts. Paredes notes that this legend is endorsed and amplified in Webb's writings and scholarship of the 1930s—from *The Great Plains* to *The Texas Rangers*—and remained uncontested until recent revisionist histories of the Southwest.

In an alternate history of the borderlands, Paredes describes how the lower Rio Grande, the Seno Mexicano, colonized by the Spanish in the mid-eighteenth century, became a refuge for spirited Native Americans who resisted Spanish rule. These free spirits were followed by colonists from the Mexican interior who migrated north in exchange for free land and freedom from government interference. This Seno Mexicano was renowned for fostering adventure and a sense of liberation, much like that associated with the West-bound pioneers north of the Rio Grande. This scenario changed with the presence of the Texas Ranger, who enforced a juridical fault line aligned with the geographical border that divided the lawful from the lawless. Thus begins the association of Mexican border crossers with criminality that would inform a series of immigration policies that transform over time to turn lawlessness into "illegality."

For Mai Ngai, the "illegal alien" is the nexus of immigration policy since World War I and the key to understanding the complex relationship of citizenship, race, and the nation-state. Restrictive immigration policies justified the intensified policing of national boundaries and borders. Indeed, the 1924 Johnson-Reed Act, the historical origin of Ngai's analysis, coincides with the inauguration of the Border Patrol, both of which mark the political shift toward migration restriction and control.[61] Nicholas De Genova examines "illegality" as a "legal production" with specific historical origins and processes traceable to post-1965 immigration legislation. Migrants caught in the immigration machine are rendered vulnerable and tractable, defined by their "deportability" and thus disposability.[62] This "illegality" is further subject to historical processes that, combined with the emergence of globalization and the decline of overt forms of racism, work together to create the cultural conditions leading to hardened immigration regimes that discriminate against immigrants, particularly those from Mexico and Central

America. The intensifying border-security regime, particularly through the expansion of Immigration and Naturalization Services' enforcement capacity, aided in the creation of "illegality."[63]

The informal system of labor migration from Mexico to the United States, formalized by the Bracero program, a World War II–era worker program that ended in the 1960s, persists to meet the agricultural industry's labor needs. This system became illegal with the 1965 Immigration and Naturalization Act, which defined Mexicans as immigrants and allotted equal quotas to all potential sending nations. Aviva Chomsky traces how this "illegality" began to accrue as the demand for labor, combined with historical patterns of migration, contradicted immigration laws that rendered migration from south of the border ever more illegal. Moreover, the condition of illegality caused seasonal labor to remain in the United States rather than to risk denial of reentry and loss of employment.[64] The legal mechanism for generating migrant illegality and deportability spatializes immigration through the possibility of removal from the domain of the nation.[65] Likewise, the association of the state surveillance apparatus with the borderlands identifies migrants with this liminal space of insecurity and suspension of rights. The space of the border shapes the status of its inhabitants and impacts the practices and procedures of the law, which, in turn, transforms immigration and border- and customs-control policy.

Threat of Context

The borderlands-policing legacy of diffusion of guilt, of punishment by proxy, distributes suspicion across migrant bodies and space so that even context incurs and shapes threat in what the contemporary military strategist Paul Rexton Kan calls, in relation to migrants fleeing narcoviolence, or "narco-refugees," the "threat of context." Kan's 2010 report for the US Army's Strategic Studies Institute describes "narco-refugees" as migrants fleeing the brutality of Mexican drug cartels. The term is instrumentalized to reshape immigration policy in a manner that inculpates the Mexican state and its emissaries for the enervation and endangering of the United States. This term signals the whole-sale integration of the security apparatus with immigration policy, while generalizing and totalizing all migrants as Mexican. The "narco-refugee" justifies the militarization of the border and the securitization of immigration.

Narco-refugees are indelibly marked by the threat they seek to escape; in the biologistic language of Kan's study, they are carriers of deadly strains of terrorism that will infect US public health, even if they are not culpable of terrorist intent. Kan deploys the term to insist on the centrality of security to immigration policy. He exhorts policy makers to "do some new thinking about the relationship between security and migration," while adumbrating several possible futures as consequences of diverse border strategies for addressing immigration, which he describes as the "narco-refugee issue."[66] The report stakes out biologism as biopolitical governmentality from the outset. The author partakes in the language of abject physicality attributed to the border zone, where migrants are described by agents as "bodies," rather than as fully constituted persons with all of the legal and political entitlements therein. From rhetoric about the declining "health of the Mexican state" and the biologism of the "blurry" border, in which "blurriness serves as a rich ecology for criminality," the immunological discourse of weakened health and infectious disease predisposes readers, in this case policy makers, to align migrants, already marked as narco-refugees, with the malignant disease of narcoterrorism as carriers of its most virulent strains.[67]

Kan notes, however, that narco-refugees are more pernicious, since as carriers, the disease is dormant and undetectable. The author likens the scenario of increased narco-refugees to Waziristan—also the site of extralegal drone strikes on the part of the United States. To describe the influx of migrants at the border, he deploys Nate Freier's term "strategic shock," in which an unanticipated, catastrophic, and unconventional force of attack causes defensive units to reorganize. In a rhetorical sleight of hand, refugees become enemy combatants waging a surprise attack. They are a "threat of context," or one that emerges without hostile design but that unintentionally generates a dangerous outcome. Kan's justification for declaring narco-refugees an ominous threat is worth quoting at some length:

> Not all refugees are benign, and the longer that they remain outside of their home country and without adequate employment, the greater the

likelihood of narco-refugees using the United States as a safe haven for violent operations southbound. Beyond just revenge killings, vigilante squads may form to return to Mexico in an attempt to clear towns of cartels and gangs. With easy access to guns in the United States, these squads could potentially conduct operations to establish condition of return of narco-refugees to Mexico. The question is whether the U.S. Government would seek to prevent or support such actions and what role the Department of Defense (DoD) or DHS would play in such a scenario.[68]

Narco-refugees, since not all are "benign," readily form sleeper cells that could become violent operatives if left without "adequate employment." Refugees become armed militia or "vigilante squads" fighting for their rightful restoration to Mexico. Kan exhorts the US government, the primary readership of his report, to develop a military strategy responsive to the narco-refugee crisis.

Kan cites Tony Payan's caution not to conflate the US "War on Drugs" and the "War on Terror" with the issue of undocumented migration ("Each problem has its own dynamics, its own actors, its own motives, its own scenarios—even when there are points of intersection among them"), only to dismiss this caution in a rhetorical sleight of hand in shifting the national context of the question. Kan contends that "the war *inside* Mexico—the war of the cartels against each other and their war against the government—is now contributing to the conflation. The violence of drug trafficking organizations is terrorizing people into migrating."[69] And these migrating bodies are bringing the threat of context into the space of the United States, conflating and confusing the regions on each side of the national dividing line to the detriment of the North. The "threat of context" spans the borderlands, justifying the binational expansion of the zone of security not just laterally across territories but vertically, through aerial dimensions. In fact, the Predator drone, fresh from Iraq and Afghanistan, had its first test deployment along the US-Mexico border in 2005. By the time Kan's report was published in 2010, drones were policing the entire US-Mexico border, providing an omniscient view while symbolizing the power of the overall surveillance infrastructure of the region, creating the optics of a border under control.

Undocumented migration occurs under the shadow of narcoterrorism and elides with all immigration as a threat to national sovereignty, a threat that must be met with force. The entire immigration apparatus is implemented as a violent strategy, rather than a screening mechanism. Security is instrumentalized as threat, a threat to the life, well-being, family integrity, and political status of the migrant. Migrants and refugees are meant to bear the burden of the trauma inflicted by these policies as necessary punishment. Borderveillant media aid and abet in this process by producing migrants as "dangerous people," evinced in the discourse around migrants as criminal agents, as "narco-refugees" and "narco-terrorists" whose mobility is aligned with the practice of "narco-terrorism" and are thus subject to preemptive security measures.

In chapter 1, I examine "borderveillant media" as the popular cultural front line of border security that emerged contemporaneously with the failures of the Secure Border Initiative (SBI) announced in 2005. The Secure Border Initiative was meant to increase surveillance at the border through an integrated system called SBI*net*, or Secure Border Initiative Network. SBI*net* promised total interoperability among agencies and a complete integration of all surveillance technologies through the Integrated Computer Assisted Detection (ICAD) database. The SBI program failed to deliver on its promise of complete technological governmentality at the border for a number of reasons. Yet one outcome of this failed initiative was the expansion of the surveillance infrastructure along the border. The various technologies introduced by this program, particularly those intended to enhance visibility—stadium lighting and mobile infrared cameras mounted on vehicles, for example—consolidated the visual surveillance capacity of the region. By the time the program was terminated in 2011, mediated forms of entertainment and wiki surveillance, or wikiveillance, had moved into the region. These include the Texas Virtual Border Watch program and reality TV shows including *Homeland Security: USA* (ABC, 2009), *Bordertown: Laredo* (A&E, 2011), *Border Wars* (National Geographic, 2010–2013), *Law on the Border* (Animal Planet, 2012), and *Border Security: America's Front Line* (National Geographic, 2016–). These media did the work that their government counterparts could not accomplish. They glorify surveillance cultures, project control of the borderlands through optical advantage, and recruit the public into supporting the practices and principles of borderveillance: screening, collecting data, and sorting migrants into split categories broadly aligned with criminal alien and domestic innocent.

Chapter 2 examines the guiding symbol of the entire borderveillant apparatus at the southern frontier: the Predator drone. The drone is the master symbol of total surveillance and data capture. It signifies a future in which military and police collaborations are carried out as local and domestic practices that veil transnational operations. The drone is invasive, capable of violating both national borders and individual privacy. Border drones extract all manner of biometric information, take video footage, and can stay aloft to keep a targeted person or area under surveillance for many hours and possibly even days. Along the border, the drone operates in a new space of sovereignty and a new frontier that is aerial and fluid. The operational role of this mechanized beast is apparent across several Customs and Border Protection strategic plans and future maps, and its cultural function is apparent in various forms of media including the docuseries *Border Wars*, Air Force recruitment videos, the TV series *Black Mirror*, Ban Lethal Autonomous Weapons' short video *Slaughterbots*, Alex Rivera's film *Sleep Dealer*, and Rivera's collaboration with Angel Nevarez on a border-drone installation called *LowDrone*. In this chapter, I argue that the drone promises a future of complete surveillance and control of mobility along the border. Yet critical cultural productions about drones expose the violence of this scenario and offer possible alternatives to the dronified future through transnational activist alliance and coordination.

Chapter 3 tackles the ecological and historical trope of the "wild border" as it relates to the politics of national security. This chapter explores the wildness of the border, or how the "wild border," as both wilderness and place of unrestricted movement, inflects immigration policy with the imaginary of the Wild West. In ecological discourses, the border is not wild enough, while according to the border-security apparatus, it is wild and beyond state control, a region where migrants move with disregard for the law. The wild border is an exceptional space where the attorney general wields power to waive environmental laws, particularly the Endangered Species Act and the National Environmental Policy Act, for the purpose of increasing border security. Yet, at the same time, migrants are inculpated as a source of ecological degradation, as interlopers on a wild scene of nature. The various meanings of "wild" in relation to the borderlands enables the surveillant infrastructure to justify migrant policing as a practice of ecological conservation. I explore the trope of the wild border as it intersects with immigration policy, ecological discourse, and the surveillant regime along the border across various media, including an episode of the Discovery Channel's *Discovery Presents* series, "Wild Border," along with the Sierra Club's short documentary called *Wild versus Wall* and aspects of other documentary "nature" media produced by the Discovery Channel and Animal Planet. Each media text lends a different valence to the "wild border," and each popularizes the justification for the expansion of the surveillant apparatus at the border.

Chapter 4 examines how border-surveillance TV shows expand their remit to include border-security shows at airport borders in "the Five Eyes"—an intelligence and security alliance among the United States, United Kingdom, New Zealand, Canada, and Australia—with plotlines similar to the border shows that take place along the US-Mexico border described in chapter 2. US border-security cultures expand outward as part of a global border optic. This worldwide border matrix delivers the global procedures, operations, and plotlines of border security through mediated forms. With ambitions even greater than the failed SBI project along US borders, the mediated cultures of border security project and endeavor to enact a future of an integrated global surveillance imaginary.

Chapter 5 engages the challenge of imagining a border future beyond surveillance. I explore several versions of the border future, from the border-security futurism of Customs and Border Protection and global border-security agencies to the future imaginaries of speculative fictions, activist work, and design models and philosophies about the border future.

The mystery of the border agent's death, described earlier, as a possible surprise attack is enhanced by the space of its occurrence. It is also a symptom of the border optic or the idea that the borderlands is an abyss of meaning and that what we see is an artifact of the histories and cultures of the region from the ideological vantage of the image maker. Agent Martinez's mysterious death, ruled an accident, elicits anxiety about the border as opaque and unknowable, in need of ever more surveillance, more transparency, and thus more control. Out of the mysterious circumstances that resulted in a Border Patrol agent's injury and death, a certainty was produced. A resolute call for the extension and fortification of the permanent wall along the border offered a simplistic remedy for the anxiety of uncertainty and fear of surprise attacks. This media event was a catalyst for increasingly phobic "zero tolerance" immigration policies and a key moment in a news cycle that elevates affect over veracity or in which affect determines veracity. This scenario exposes the workings of the entire border-security apparatus as a new form of racial capitalism, one that operates through the techniques and technologies of frontier surveillance. The racial logic of White supremacy shapes the cultural production of race at the border in which "Americanness" is defined by proximity to Whiteness.[70] The media spectacle of the Border Patrol death adds another layer to this racial dynamic; it reveals the uneasy intersection of security and race in which the citizen subject, in this case Agent Martinez, is defined less by racial or ethnic contours than by his alliance with the surveillance state, one that serves to maintain White power and entitlements.

Media about the border disseminate a culture of borderveillance and mark the integration of immigration surveillance with entertainment modes. Control over mobility, along with the procedures of processing and sorting migrants into citizen and noncitizen, is not merely a news event local to the border regions but part of the drama of everyday life in the United States. *Border Optics* explores this expansive surveillant gaze and refocalizes it to expose the inherent failures of and resistance to the borderveillant apparatus that would visually apprehend and control migrants out of fear and anxiety about loss of territory and White dominion. Resistance to the surveillant apparatus at the border reminds us that these technologies are neither inevitable nor infallible. Moreover, this story of technology is challenged by new figurations, metaphors, symbologies, and fictions about the border and its future, many of which are part of the history of the region and might be resuscitated and reinvigorated to new ends.

1

Borderveillant Media

What it comes down to is a consequence. If there's no conse-
quence for these people, they'll continue to do it.
—Michael Lee, Border Patrol agent on *Border Wars*
(Nat Geo)

Borderveillance describes the operations of a vast network and infrastructure of oversight, control, and management of regions that
symbolize the bounded and secured nation, marking these regions as
permanent fields of the visible. It signals a booming security-industrial
complex that includes entertainment media, local and federal policing,
prisons and detention centers, the aerospace industry, and all manner
of security-technology industries. Surveillance of migrants is a lucra-
tive endeavor that justifies the expansion of invasive techniques of
social control of all populations, mobile and settled. The entire drama
of borderveillance infuses everyday life, flowing to territories beyond the
border through various forms of media. Borderveillance media are the
popular front line of the entire culture and politics of border enforcement, which includes strategic studies, policy recommendations, news
reports, and congressional hearings. These media produce the experience of viewing as sorting by training the viewer to detect anomalies,
people and things, that must be detained at the border for the sake of
national security. The migrant is not simply a risk to but an enemy of the
state. Mobile populations are, in a manner described by James Scott, a
"thorn in the side of the state." For Scott, modern statecraft is a project of
sustaining state legibility and boundedness through ambitious top-down
planning that requires "seeing like a state."[1] Borderveillant spectatorship
is a proxy for the state, for immigration and customs enforcement in
which viewership involves screening and sorting of mobile populations,
not just at the border but across the entire nation and, ultimately, the
world.

Entertainment media about southern border security gained programming traction after a key policy change called "enforcement with consequences," formalized and implemented in 2011 as the Consequence Delivery System (CDS) and described in the *2012–2016 Border Patrol Strategic Plan* as enabling Border Patrol to "manage, as opposed to simply react to, the volume of illegal traffic along our borders through the application of appropriate consequences to illegal entrants."[2] The policy of enforcement with consequences aimed to "improve detection and removal capacity" and hinder unauthorized migration with stricter penalties to put an official end to "catch and release" policies and shift away from "prevention through deterrence" policies.[3] Instead of informal returns, migrants faced a range of consequences, including formal removal, prosecution, repatriation, and notices to appear in court. The CDS would apply metrics to standardize and automate decision-making, ridding subjective human deliberations from security procedures to ensure that consequences are delivered effectively and resources are allocated accordingly. It should be noted, however, that the strategy of prevention through deterrence has lasting impact: it shuttled migrants to precarious routes away from urban centers and into dangerous and inhospitable terrain, effectively weaponizing migration corridors. The policy of enforcement with consequences transformed borderland communication networks through technocratic means that enhanced the biopolitical governmentality of the border region, that is, by emphasizing public health and safety or the logic of preemption over the logic of deterrence.

The Consequence Delivery System replaced the Secure Border Initiative's operational strategy of prevention through deterrence. The Secure Border Initiative (SBI) had several iterations, formerly called the Integrated Surveillance Information System (ISIS) in the late 1990s and then renamed America's Shield Initiative (ASI). The latter was incorporated into SBI and renamed SBI*net* Technology in the early 2000s. The Secure Border Initiative expanded the security infrastructure at the border with the development of new surveillance technologies that would form part of an integrated system called SBI*net*.[4] It was under SBI that the first UAVs were deployed along the southern border as part of a larger system of imagined interoperability among agencies and a complete coordination of all surveillance technologies through the Integrated Computer Assisted Detection database (ICAD). Surveillance capacity was expanded with various technologies including remote video surveillance, radars, and ground sensors, combined with tactical infrastructure for enhanced visibility through stadium lighting and mobile infrared cameras mounted on various kinds of vehicles and expanded communication networks through the creation of roads and vehicle pathways. Under SBI*net*, the border would finally be fully managed, monitored, and defended by a virtual technological barrier.[5]

This future never came to pass. The Department of Homeland Security terminated SBI*net* in 2011 for overall failure due to cost overruns, delays, and technical problems—notably the same year that CDS was implemented. The cancellation of this expansive integrated surveillance plan dashed the promise of complete technocratic governmentality along the southwestern border. Yet technology and infrastructure remained the key to border security. In the congressional review of the failed SBI*net* program, technology remains integral to future plans: "Technology has really been an integral part of the proposed solution to secure the vast and rugged terrain of the Southwest Border for a long time, and it is one part of an overall set of solutions that must include manpower, intelligence, and where appropriate, infrastructure."[6]

Though the SBI*net* program failed, its objectives, part of "the overall DHS goal of protecting the United States from dangerous people, and the related objective of achieving effective control of U.S. borders," have continued through other techniques and technologies of surveillance.[7] These include mediated cultures of surveillance and technology plans to secure the border with UAVs, integrated fixed towers equipped with radar and day and night cameras, ground sensors, and mobile long-range night-vision scopes—in short, all of the functional aspects of the SBI plan.[8] The Consequence Delivery System deemphasized a monolithic approach to security and reduced "reliance on any single point or program," while extending the "zone of security" beyond US territorial borders. It expanded border surveillance to the entirety of the nation, with the idea that "overarching border security efforts require a whole-of-government approach that emphasizes the importance of joint planning and intelligence sharing."[9]

The SBI policy initiatives, even if full integration was never realized, amplified the televisuality of the US Southwest borderlands by adding new technologies that make the spectacle of border security more dramatic. Also, as surveillance capacity expands, the ways of crossing the border and evading detection proliferate, and as consequences for violating security protocol intensify, so do the elements of drama, including intrigue, tension, and suspense. This repetition, with varying levels of innovation, became the basis of formulaic, cost-efficient, high-volume reality TV series. The growth of surveillance capacity begets the expansion of a surveillance culture and its spectacular scenes and plotlines. A number of serialized TV shows do the work that the DHS's integrated surveillance programs failed to accomplish: they project total visual and informational control of the border and recruit public participation in and support of border-surveillance initiatives. They do so, in part, by aligning border-patrol story lines with the classic fictional genre of the western. This symbolic gesture cultivates audiences attuned to the genre, while it promotes ideas at cross-purposes with the technocratic aspirations of the Department of Homeland Security. These shows, as modern westerns, are premised on the importance of human and animal resources as privileged borderland denizens imbued with skill and intuition, over the role of machines and technology as sites of automation and signs of automatic security. This bio-logic is key to the overarching symbolic story line and continual refrain of border security as a "cat and mouse" game. Furthermore, in borderveillant media, human preeminence over machines is part of the humanitarian alibi of the border-surveillance regime.

Borderveillant TV shows transform an actual webcam surveillance "virtual community watch" program, the Texas Virtual Border Watch Program, into consumable entertainment. The webcam program, piloted in 2006, began in November 2008 as a private corporate partnership of BlueServo with the state of Texas. Through the BlueServo website interface, connected to cameras along the US-Mexico border, anyone can participate in border patrol as a form of "wikiveillance," or crowdsourced security.[10]

This form of participatory media shapes new ways of thinking about the intersection of power, technology, and citizenship in a neoliberal era. By crowdsourcing security, private citizens become responsible to the Border Patrol, and responsibilities replace rights in the definition of citizen.[11] Ultimately the public is rendered docile in the reproduction of

Figure 1.1. BlueServo sponsors wikiveillance, or crowdsourced border surveillance. (BlueServo, "Actual Sighting Videos—BorderWatch Archives," accessed June 14, 2020, www.blueservo.com)

hegemonic power relations and performs the work of national-security vigilantism. Luis Figueroa, an attorney with the Mexican American Legal and Educational Defense Fund, called the Texas Virtual Border Watch Program "almost a state-funded vigilante program."[12] According to the BlueServo website, the public participates in "border surveillance" by reporting over email: "The Public, acting as Virtual Texas Deputies[SM], is limited to reporting suspicious activities via email. Local county Sheriffs will respond to these reports, conduct all investigations, and take appropriate actions. This service will provide millions of dollars in benefits to local border Sheriffs, with the public acting as additional pairs of eyes for Deputies on the ground. This extra surveillance will allow the public to directly participate in reducing crime and improving their communities. It is a well-established fact that citizen involvement in community watch programs such as this one reduces crime."[13] This program was a popular form of surveillance entertainment, at least initially, as a civic duty in a kind of armchair civilian border-defense initiative like others of its ilk, with some people acting as vigilantes and others impersonating Border Patrol agents; these include the Minutemen Project,

Ranch Rescue, Border Rescue, American Border Patrol, Americans for Zero Immigration, Civil Homeland Defense, Arizona Patriots, and United Constitutional Patriots.[14] The latter two groups use the Facebook livestream feature as a form of surveillance media to broadcast their vigilante activities. Activists for undocumented migrants also use this and other platforms and apps to document and expose Border Patrol and ICE violations. The nativist vigilante groups recall the early history of the Texas Rangers as a volunteer protopolicing group committed to the defense of the state against unlawful intruders.

The Texas Virtual Border Watch Program was popular but ultimately ineffective, falling far short of its stated objectives and goals. The program intended to work with private landowners to place cameras in hundreds of locations, yet by 2010, there were only twenty-nine cameras and twenty-six arrests attributable to the program. It was followed by a nonpublic surveillance system, Operation Drawbridge, which exploits the border deconstitutionalized zone to place cameras on private land. This program exploited access to private land for border-security purposes through a provision of the Immigration and Nationality Act:

> Any officer or employee of the Service authorized under regulations prescribed by the Attorney General shall have power without warrant:
> . . . within a reasonable distance from any external boundary of the United States, to board and search for aliens any vessel within the territorial waters of the United States and any railway car, aircraft, conveyance, or vehicle, and within a distance of twenty-five miles from any such external boundary to have access to private lands, but not dwellings, for the purpose of patrolling the border to prevent the illegal entry of aliens into the United States. (8 USC 1357)

The hundred-mile rule allows agents to conduct "reasonable searches," and without "reasonable cause," they must obtain warrants to search vehicles.[15] The quoted provision allows for access to land for border security. Other provisions are exploited for analog security in the region, particularly the Fifth Amendment, which enables the government to use private land for public works, for example, to build the border wall, under eminent domain.

The web-based wiki and Border Watch site may have failed to meet their objectives, but they succeeded in establishing viewing habits that fostered an audience for similar surveillance entertainment. Though the Texas Virtual Border Watch resulted in few actual apprehensions, it elicited the curiosity of large numbers of voyeurs ready for more dramatic migrant surveillance. Unlike the unmediated view from the webcam, which might yield hours of uneventful footage, borderveillant reality TV adds plot to action to intensify the pace of policing, to guide the spectator with narration, and to piece together disparate events into a story line and insert them into a moral universe. These story lines coincide with state discourses and a military strategy of preparedness against "surprise attacks" by an enemy alien who might use the ruse of undocumented entry to unsettle the state.

A number of borderveillance docuseries about crime on the border capture a cultural moment of intensifying border security; they exploit a market created by other shows about law enforcement, the Texas Virtual Border Watch Program, the long arc of and shadow of the western genre tradition, and a phobic cultural climate linking migration with the influx of "dangerous people" across US borders. These shows include *Homeland Security: USA* (ABC, 2009), *Bordertown: Laredo* (A&E, 2011), *Border Wars* (National Geographic, 2010–2013), *Law on the Border* (Animal Planet, 2012), and *Border Security: America's Front Line* (National Geographic, 2016–). They evoke ideas about risk management and immigration and allude to issues of identity protection and data security. They train audiences in security protocols, not so that they might act on behalf of the state as protopolice agents—which occurs only in some cases—but more generally to acculturate public audiences to visual codes that ground the mood of suspicion and anxiety in practical scenarios that justify the violence of immigration policy, often masquerading as humanitarianism, and to garner public support. Borderveillant media narrate one side of the border-security dynamic, and while reality TV shows attempt to repress or deny migrants' realities, a story of resistance and refusal finds its way into the visual frame. This chapter explores the ubiquity and force of the cultural mood of surveillance, exposing its way of seeing, while seeking moments of disruption that contest the imperious narrative and logic of Immigration and Customs Enforcement (ICE) and border security.

Borderveillance Cultures

SBI*net* may have failed, but its promise of infrastructural compre-
hensiveness has remained an objective of the Department of Homeland
Security. The United States Government Accountability Office (GAO)
issued a report, one of sixteen such reports on the SBI program, that
detailed the failures of the program, along with "observations on the
importance of applying lessons learned to future projects."[16] Perhaps
the key "lesson" acquired in the pilot project for SBI*net*, called Project
28 under contract with Boeing, emanated from "lack of user involvement" in design and development or a mismatch between developers
and people in the field, Border Patrol agents and officials. Border
Patrol agents reported numerous system deficiencies and bemoaned
not being involved sooner in the process. Many of the new technologies hindered, due to design failure, rather than aided or enhanced
Border Patrol work.

This scenario resounds with the plot of the 1984 border film *Flashpoint*, in which freewheeling agents are downsized by technology, effectively replaced by ground sensors and relegated to desk jobs in a plan
devised by out-of-touch federal agents. *Flashpoint* is one of a few Hollywood border films from the 1980s, an era of immigrant fears and phobia,
including *Borderline* (1980) and *The Border* (1982), that are about male
Border Patrol agents as modern-day cowboys and honest workingmen
beset and beleaguered by the consequences of inadequate policy and
insufficient government funding.[17] These cinematic heroes set the visual
and ethical terms for agents as humane and skilled borderland denizens who know well, better than outsiders to the region, the land and
the people that they surveil. They expose a chasm between the cowboy
agents on the ground and the technocracy in Washington, DC, in a manner that aligns Border Patrol agents with the migrants they apprehend.
In some cases, these hardworking border cops supplant undocumented
migrants as the "real" victims of neoliberal globalization, victims whose
stories demand to be told.

Hollywood border films about CBP agents are antecedent to the
current slate of border-patrol media, from mainstream to alternative,
that put Border Patrol agents at the helm and fulcrum of story lines
to humanize the ongoing efforts of border surveillance and security

and make them appear as sympathetic workers beset by state policies rather than embodiments of them. In fact, the premise of *Border Wars*, the most popular of the border-security reality TV series, according to Nicholas Stein, the show's producer, is to tell border agents' untold stories and show the dangers and risks they face without "talking policy," to humanize agents without any reference to the historical or political context of enforcement. These shows present policing as ever more difficult and irksome labor in response to threats that are intensifying and becoming more complex. The series frames border-patrol labor as hard, honest, and humanitarian work that protects migrants and ensures the welfare and security of the nations on both sides of the US-Mexico border. This dynamic relationship deflects attention from the institutional and political structure of the immigration apparatus, in which the United States participates in the conditions that cause migration. Stein, in an interview on KPBS Public Broadcasting, describes the mission of the show:

> Now when we got involved with these agents and officers, we told them— and this is what we did—which was, we were there to tell their story.
>
> We were there to pull back the curtain and let people see exactly what it's like day to day, car by car, mission by mission, shift by shift, what it's really like to try to secure the U.S.-Mexico border. And in many ways Nogales became a microcosm, if you will, of some of the issues and problems that are up and down all the way from San Diego all the way to Brownsville, Texas. So it's a real look at the work and the dedication of the men and women there. We didn't talk policy, we didn't talk about, you know, what people should do in terms of policy and legislation and laws. We were there with the law enforcers and we saw how difficult their job really is.[18]

The show is about individual stories of policing that are emblematic of the entire national-security apparatus. *Border Wars* and shows of the procedural borderlands police genre deflect the "human interest" story of immigration onto that of the Border Patrol agents, often also immigrants or racialized subjects, to tell stories of their travails and tragedies to co-opt public pathos for the downtrodden and the marginal. This is accomplished in part through memorializing agents who were killed in action and through a recurrent emphasis on the cyclical nature of the endlessly enervating labors of Border Patrol agents. They are blue-collar humanitarian workers defined by the virtues of sacrifice, will, and dedication.

The stakes of border-patrol work, according to this and other border-security shows, are intensified by the responsibilities inherent to the project of national defense, with the latter marking its difference from local police work. Stein makes the national-security implications of *Border Wars* part of what distinguishes it from police reality TV shows like *Cops*:

> I want to make one quick distinction there because I've certainly had many friends and colleagues who've worked on law enforcement shows like "Cops" and others that are done right here domestically. What I found so interesting about working law enforcement on the border is that everything about that is different than, say, watching crime in Baltimore and Newark or Cleveland or goodness knows where because everything that happens at the border, even though some of it involves some of the same law enforcement techniques, has enormous implications, you know, has enormous security implications, immigration implications. You know, every single person that tries to come in here illegally, they're worried about terrorism. They're worried about so many things, and it brings up so many emotions and issues that it really, to me, I just found it—and I still find it—just endlessly interesting even though some of the action, like you say, is like "Cops." But the international piece of it and the border protection piece of it just has layer after layer after layer of complexity, heartbreaking immigration stories, you know, stories about what it means to be an American, what it means to be a Mexican, what it means to be a Honduran or Guatemalan or all—these folks are coming from everywhere.[19]

Though Stein is describing *Border Wars*, he could be stating the objective of any one of the reality TV shows about the border. The show reveals border police work to an uninitiated audience through its "enormous security implications," which, unlike domestic policing, operate within an international context. The differentiation of local and federal enforcement obscures the reality of increasing militarization of local police forces and the expansion of police work as border-patrol support, dramatized and normalized in other shows of the genre, notably *Law on the Border* and *Bordertown: Laredo.*

The use of the military along the border has a long history; more recently, it is a consequence of the Defense Authorization Act of 1982. In 1989, as part of President H. W. Bush's National Drug Control Strategy, the military set up the El Paso–based Joint Task Force 6 (JTF-6), composed of active-duty US military forces, to participate in anti-drug-trafficking campaigns along the southern border. These efforts dissolved what remained of the boundary separating domestic from foreign military enforcement.[20] The act expanded support for all federal law enforcement agencies to provide operation, intelligence, engineering, and general support, in other words, to apply military-grade surveillance capacity to the Border Patrol. The Joint Task Force facilitated this coordination with the expansion of infrastructure through road construction, lighting, fencing, and barriers. Its remit and territorial area of operation included the expanse of the US-Mexico borderlands within a fifty-mile extension, as well as borderized areas including the Texas Gulf Coast, Houston, and Los Angeles.[21]

The Joint Task Force works closely with the Border Patrol along the border in a manner similar to its predecessor, BORTAC (Border Patrol Tactical Unit), created in 1984. BORTAC, with special paramilitary training, applies SWAT (special weapons and tactics) practices to the borderlands. BORTAC has a unique mandate; it operates nationally with a global orientation and responsibility to train border forces in other regions of the world.[22] Todd Miller calls BORTAC the "U.S. Border Patrol's robocops." In its "global response capability," it trains and supervises border agents beyond the United States and aids in globalizing US border-security tactics in Afghanistan, Argentina, Armenia, Belize, Colombia, Costa Rica, Ecuador, Guatemala, Haiti, Honduras, Jordan, Kenya, Kosovo, Mexico, Panama, Peru, Tajikistan, and Ukraine.[23] Though BORTAC's headquarters are in El Paso, Texas, there are members throughout the United States who might be called on for immediate deployment for special purposes, particularly "high-risk warrant service; intelligence, reconnaissance and surveillance; foreign law enforcement/Border Patrol capacity building; airmobile operations; maritime operations; and precision marks-man/observer."[24]

In the episode "Contraband Highway" of *Border Wars*, a BORTAC team is deployed to "bolster" security and perform a special mission to stake out drug-trafficking border routes. The team is sent to surveil a suspicious white truck, but the mission yields little more than vehicle and driver information. The BORTAC team relays these data to the Border Patrol and moves on to another mission somewhere along the two-thousand-mile border. BORTAC training and supervision intensifies the militarization of the US perimeter and disseminates its border principles all over the world, in a manner congruent with US security initiatives and policies. Border-surveillance media introduce these innovations to a wider public, not just in the United States but across global media markets (discussed in greater detail in chapter 4).

Borderveillance media are national-security entertainment with a regular cast of characters of good Border Patrol agents—as national defense agents and humanitarian workers—and impoverished migrants, deemed "illegal" and thus rendered ever more vulnerable to corruption and criminality. Border and customs officials treat border crossers and all those who appear at ports of entry as suspect of deceit or traffic in contraband. It is up to the agents and their proxies, viewers, to discern the difference between a migrant seeking lawful or unauthorized entry and a narcotrafficker. This mission deflects from the actual work of borderveillant media, reflecting both policy and public discourse, to demonstrate that this divide is ultimately blurred and that all migrants are potential narcoterrorists. This is evident across several story lines about otherwise-law-abiding migrants who are tricked or coerced into working for traffickers.

Border Wars and all of the border-security reality TV shows tell the untold story of Border Patrol agents' work to mythologize them as key players in immigration control as a national-security objective. Immigration and Customs Enforcement and Border Patrol agents are not merely processing people seeking entry to the United States; they are defending the nation. The culture of surveillance, including the reality TV shows about border security, contradicts the engineering ideology of border infrastructure projects in which integrated technological systems of command, control, communication, surveillance, and detection work to supplement, enhance, and, in some cases, supplant border agents on the ground. These shows emphasize human and animal skills over new surveillant technologies by privileging human over machine, often by underscoring the uniquely animalistic characteristics of agents and police, notable by their nicknames, like Mario López, aka "Falcon," in *Law on the Border*, or through individual intuition, experience, intelligence, and humanitarian or humane aid. These shows renew the borderlands mythos of cowboys, Rangers, and Border Patrol agents as heroes of western lore whose know-how cannot be replicated by machines. The machines have a different role. They cast the entire borderlands under the shadow of surveillance to create the mood of a controlled environment, but the truly effective and optimal method of individual capture and detention is mammalian and analog, a game of cat and mouse.

Cat and Mouse Game

In Cheech Marin's comedic send-up of the immigration regime, the film *Born in East L.A.* (1987), the border-control apparatus is ridiculed as a game. Rudy Robles is mistaken for an undocumented immigrant and deported to Mexico despite being a US citizen. Though Rudy adapts to his new circumstances, he finds a way to return to the United States but not before he turns several attempts to cross the border into games of strategy. The US-defined dynamics and values associated with the players are reversed. Rudy is told that the "bad guys" are those in the green-and-white trucks, the Border Patrol, and that "pollos" must evade them and try to make it across an open field to the coyotes. Rudy coaches prospective "pollos" with a playbook of various diagrammed tactical plays for making it across the field. The scene is accompanied by the sound of a crowd cheering while Rudy rushes the field, only to be tackled by a Border Patrol agent as a whistle blows. In another play, Rudy wears an entire camouflage bush on his back, complete with cactus and other plants, making progress north by running and crouching every few feet. When Border Patrol exits the scene, he unburdens himself of the camouflage bush and makes a break for it. When Border Patrol returns, he dives into a bush, belatedly discovering that it is attached to the back of a Border Patrol truck. In each of these tactical plays, the Border Patrol exerts strategic advantage that thwarts Rudy's individual efforts. For Rudy to transform his circumstances, his tactic must be popular, a mass movement, and political. The final scene shows Rudy marching forth across the border with massive numbers of migrants whose final strategy is political visibility, accompanied by the demands of cultural citizenship—evident when Rudy, crossing by underground tunnel, reemerges onto the streets of San Diego into the middle of a Cinco de Mayo parade.

Border policing has a ritual effect akin to a spectator sport, keenly dramatized in *Born in East L.A.* The notion of the "game" is used to present border security as a dynamic that the US government, with various strategic advantages, is fated to win. Peter Andreas describes security along the border in similar terms as "border games," emphasizing the vicissitudes of policing that shift according to political gaming. Andreas notes that while the 1990s marked the opening of the border through the North American Free Trade Agreement (NAFTA), it was also an era that witnessed the doubling of the size of the US Border Patrol and thus the tightening of border security. The border was open to trade but closed to migrants and illicit drugs, or what Andreas notes is the concurrence of a "borderless economy" and a "barricaded border" that is part of the strategic representation to remake the image of the border as the ultimate sign of state sovereignty.[25]

Andreas uses the metaphor of the "game" in lieu of prevailing metaphors of war, natural disaster, or crises like "invasion" or "flood" and thus highlights the dynamism of enforcement and the strategic dynamic between agents and migrants. Like Rachel Hall's transparent traveler, border games are premised on a performance of security and risk that presupposes the presence of spectators and in which the borderlands is the arena of sport. Border security is a game, a sporting event with teams or groups pit against each other in a manner that indexes the transnational dynamics of sports. Border reality TV shows use the language of the game but with different symbolic resonance. These shows describe border security as a "cat and mouse" game, which emphasizes individual efforts outside of a larger political or cultural sphere and draws on a species hierarchy that connotes values related to the privileges and entitlements of domestication or naturalization or a tacit divide between the native or naturalized citizen, the cat, and the unwanted guest, the mouse.

Border security is a "cat and mouse" game premised on a Manichean dynamic of good agent versus potential terrorist that veils an ever-expanding market for security technologies and surplus material, people and things, from foreign conflicts. National Geographic's *Border Wars* describes this dynamic as a "kind of battleground" where a "high stakes game of cat and mouse is played out between those who want to cross the border illegally and those whose job it is to stop them" (season 1, episode 1). This exact phrasing is replicated in the narration for a show on a competing cable network, *Animal Planet*, in its own version of the border reality TV show, called *Law on the Border*. The narration intones, "Their country and their jobs are completely defined by the border fence. It's a boundary, a gateway, and a target for the Mexican cartel and their smugglers. In this high-stakes game of cat and mouse, they'll do anything to go through, over, or even under it" (season 1, episode 1). Likewise, in *Bordertown: Laredo*, cops who have a suspected drug stash house under surveillance describe their plan as a "sit and wait, basically a cat and mouse" (season 1, episode 2), and in *Border Security: America's Front Line* (season 1, episode 6), the narration intones that "for CBP officers catching smugglers is a tactical game of cat and mouse."

The various reality TV series about border surveillance are based on the rehearsal of the performance of security along with repetition of the predominant theme of the "cat and mouse" game. This repetition routinizes border-security practices and makes them appear natural, part of the agonistic dynamics of the animal kingdom. The idea of border security as a "cat and mouse" game functions to depoliticize the border region and minimizes the violence inherent to border policy and its security practices. The "mouse," or the migrant, is part of a game of chase and an emblem of the entire immigration apparatus and a criminalized category. This idiom is based in a logic of predator and prey as simply part of the cycle of nature, that is, natural rather than ideological or the result of political dynamics between the United States and Mexico. The entire mediated landscape of migration is based in this endless cyclical and circular loop in which beleaguered protectors of the US homeland defend against invasive and unwanted species. The symbolic hue of this constant refrain of "cat and mouse"—again, repeated in each series by a number of Border Patrol agents, police, and narrators—attributes diminished value to the chased, the mice, who are, as Art Spiegelman conveyed in his graphic allegory about the Holocaust, *Maus*, persecuted by cats, by cruel and predatory animal actors in a genocidal tale. The idiom "cat and mouse" in these reality TV series is deployed in a way that never quite builds to a fable; rather, it alludes to the chase that is doomed to repetition in the mold of the iconic US American slapstick cat and mouse cartoon, *Tom and Jerry*. Spiegelman's fable lays bare the existential values in the hierarchy of species in which the powerful and nimble predators exert dominion over abject and powerless prey. Moreover, *Maus* rids the animal metaphor of any ludic or slapstick connotations. The symbolic language that aligns denigrated populations with vermin or pests is prevalent in regimes of racial capitalism in which hierarchies of race and ethnicity are rigidly defined.

Border media have a genocidal referent embedded in their discourse: the history of the "settling" of the West and the Southwest is one of ethnic cleansing. Gary Clayton Anderson explores how Native Tejanos and Native Americans were integral to the consolidation of the Texan state, yet they were subject to a state-endorsed policy of ethnic cleansing and dispossession on principles of xenophobia and White supremacy: "Why, then, did most Anglos come to condemn Indians and Tejanos despite their important economic contributions? The dominant Anglos had a cultural justification for their racism—non-Anglo ethnic groups possessed different languages, different dress, different economies, and different religions—in short, different cultures that Anglos marginalized in terms of their value. The justification for attacks upon such non-Anglo groups evolved out of an imagined fear that such groups would somehow pollute what Anglos perceived as their superior culture. Nonconformity to an Anglo-southern culture offered the ultimate rationale for the seizure of Indian and Tejano land and property."[26]

The border-security shows do not acknowledge the violent history of the Southwest; rather, the institutionalized racial animus born of an earlier era is deflected by the alibi of a majority Latinx workforce—all in the service of a culture and system that sustain White supremacy and nationalism. The figurative language of "cat and mouse" encodes a racial logic hidden in the story line and obscured by a diverse cast of characters. Nationality and citizenship status are privileged over racial affiliation. There is no racial division across national lines; that is, Latinxs constitute Border Patrol agents and the patrolled alike. CBP agents act to protect both migrants' welfare and the nation; they are often of the communities they police and emphasize their "love of their country" and nativist desire to protect it, or as Mario López, aka Falcon, of the canine unit in Nogales describes his domain, "Nogales, Arizona, it's a small community. It's my home town. I was born and raised here. This is America, you know. Love my country" (season 1, episode 1). In some cases, agents describe their complicated relationship to policing people with whom they share a heritage, but they ultimately revert to the idea that their responsibility, and thus alliance, is to their country.

The more complex "reality" of these shows reflects the borderlands' social and political conditions, premised on the typology of citizen and alien, cat and mouse, or what Zygmunt Bauman calls the difference between "tourist" and "vagabond"—the latter is criminalized and, along the border, racialized.[27] This scenario plays into the current atmosphere of immigrant phobia, in which citizenship status as "legal" supplants racial difference at the same time that it continues to stand in for it. That is, Latinx citizens are defined as "legal" against "illegal" noncitizens, or what Michelle Alexander notes is the "new caste system" of the criminal justice system, in which race is coded as criminal and criminals are subject to legally sanctioned forms of discrimination, denial of rights, and social exclusion that were common during the Jim Crow era of segregation.[28] In borderveillant media, US citizens are protagonists in story lines that partake in the western, a genre imbued with the history of the racial violence of the region.

The Shadow of the Western

Southwestern borderveillance docuseries are part of a media tradition at the intersection of history, reporting, and entertainment under the long shadow the region's prevailing genre, the classical western. Many of the tropes of the classical western, from the cowboys-and-Indians conflict narratives, captivity tales, and stories of rampaging and rapacious bandits, infuse the story lines and voice-over narrations of the docuseries on border security. These shows are part of the history of mediated borderlands that include all manner of westerns, from classical to modern, and more recent serialized shows, particularly those related to drug trafficking, including *Kingpin* (NBC, 2003), *Weeds* (Showtime, 2005–2012), *Breaking Bad* (AMC, 2008–2013), *Queen of the South* (USA Network, 2016–), and *Better Call Saul* (AMC 2015–) and the Hollywood films *Traffic* (2000), *No Country for Old Men* (2007), *The Three Burials of Melquiades Estrada* (2006), and the *Sicario* film series (2015, 2018). These story lines link drug trafficking to the borderlands, while the dramatic tension of migrant narratives in Hollywood—for instance, *El Norte* (1984), *Mi Familia / My Family* (1995), and *Under the Same Moon* (2007)—emanates from the sense that the migrant journey occurs in the shadow of illegality. The reality TV shows about the border transform the major tropes of the border story lines from the unauthorized movement of goods and people to increased surveillance and the pervasiveness of security technologies to redefine the border genre as an effect of surveillance culture. The latter outcome is presciently framed by Alex Rivera in his film *Sleep Dealer* (2008), discussed in chapter 2, which features surveillance of dissidents along the border and a spirited cross-border alliance formed to undermine this regime.

Border reality television series are a response to the increased interest in policing and surveillance at the border and national ports of entry. These shows appeal to audiences seeking participation in the action of border security by creating a sense of immediacy and urgency within a procedural drama that typically ends with the apprehension of a suspect or suspects or of contraband goods. Borderveillant media follow the procedures of law-and-order shows, in which the audience identifies with the honorable agent of the law and engages in all parts of the action leading up to an arrest. To the extent that some of these shows are surveillance media and use surveillance camera footage from the border-security apparatus, they are part of a genre of crime TV and its prehistory of closed-circuit television (CCTV) surveillance.

Clive Norris and Gary Armstrong note a coalescing of cameras and crime in the rapid growth of CCTV systems in the 1990s in Britain. The presence of cameras in public spaces was framed by the media as a public good and an effective method of combating crime. Norris and Armstrong argue, "Television is a visual medium. CCTV is a visual medium. They were made for each other. Add one other ingredient, crime, and you have the perfect marriage. A marriage that can blur the distinction between entertainment and news; between documentary and spectacle and between voyeurism and current affairs."[29] British crime shows in the 1990s regularly used CCTV footage to add veracity and drama. These shows then sustained public support for the expansion of the surveillance apparatus into ever more public spaces, toward the creation of the "maximum surveillance society."[30]

Borderveillant shows aid and abet the work of the state. Drawing on Foucault's analysis of governmentality, Peter Hughes describes the Australian version of the global *Border Security* series, *Border Security: Australia's Front Line*, as a successful "instrument of governmentality" that promotes the work of national-security agencies and mobilizes public support for it.[31] These shows are a hybrid mix of documentary, entertainment media, and public-relations promotional vehicles. They dramatize the efforts of liberal governing, in which the management of populations occurs at a distance, rather than through direct or authoritarian rule. State recognition of individual rights and liberties means that populations must be acculturated to forms of self-rule. One such form, according to Laurie Ouellette and James Hay, occurs through the plotlines and through lines of reality television shows that "assess and guide the ethics, behaviors, aspirations, and routines of ordinary people."[32] Reality television offers "guides" for social comportment, whereas in these national-security shows, particularly those that take place in airports, a major goal is improving public relations with agencies of national security. Lifestyle reality television programming offers informal guides for living a proper life within the responsibilities and bounds of good citizenship.

Borderveillance reality programming is more in line with procedural law enforcement genres—from reality to fictional—which disseminate actual policies and legal guidelines that educate and acculturate viewers to a national-security regime. Yet reality shows of all genres share a common addressee, the citizen, who is hailed as responsible for self-empowerment and capable of identifying and sorting populations along legal lines regarding immigration status. This idea of seeing and sorting, of identifying and targeting people, anticipates and coincides with the "see something, say something" campaign launched in 2010 by the Department of Homeland Security. In Joshua Reeves's account of civic responsibility and state surveillance, he argues that this program set the terms for a post-9/11 surveillance state in which all citizens are implicated and responsible. Much like the Texas Virtual Border Watch Program, civic programs like the National Neighborhood Watch (1972), the 911 crime-reporting apparatus (1968), and DARE (Drug Abuse

Resistance Education, 1981) create a culture of citizen responsibility and "participatory political culture" aimed at internal communities of the United States.[33] The emphasis is less on the technologies and techniques of the security apparatus than on its human resources.

Borderveillance media are addressed to an internal citizenry, while they target external populations. Audiences are encouraged to identify with agents so that they might appreciate the overwhelming magnitude and cyclical nature of border-security labors and empathize with Border Patrol agents' aggrieved state of overwork. Rather than resist or resent scrutiny and review, audiences might more readily adhere to security protocol at national borders, ports of entry, and other sites of policing. Furthermore, before preparing to travel, they might undergo a process of self-surveillance and reduce or remove any appearance of anomaly, thereby diminishing agents' labors.

Borderveillant shows meet a public desire to see and know how various US borders are monitored and patrolled according to the policies and technologies of the Department of Homeland Security. *Border Wars*, in season 4, reveals the machinery of surveillance when it dispenses with the mediation of framing to depict an unredacted aerial view from Border Patrol surveillance cameras. Images of the border fence from the surveillance center in downtown Nogales provide much of the visual landscape of the show. The surveillance feed ceases to be framed to become an unmediated view, accompanied by voice-over narration and police description of the scene. The *Border Wars* camera then shifts to the cityscape "outside of camera range," or more precisely, outside of the surveillance-camera range in Nogales but well within the show's visual frame. Just beyond the surveillance camera, agents wait to apprehend undocumented border crossers, while the camera captures a sweeping aerial view of the border fence before landing "back at the crime scene." The procedures of criminal detection, arrest, and forensics are complete, signaled by a return to the command center, where an agent watches the entire scene unfold on his computer. This visual trick conveys the greater surveillance power of the show, one that is abetted by agents on the ground. In both the limited scope of the surveillance center and the show's expanded camera view, the scene is viewed from above, from a perspective that asserts the omniscience of state power, bolstered and enhanced by borderveillant media.

Borderveillant media offer the drama of the state in practice, exposing its logic and operational structure and making it appealing for its humane dimensions. For instance, Border Patrol agents administer aid in the form of food, water, and medical attention that may save the life of a migrant in precarious physical conditions. In one case, an undocumented migrant under suspicion of trafficking drugs is shot several times by Mexican agents as he escapes to the northern side of the Rio Grande. He is found by US Border Patrol agents, who work quickly to staunch his wounds and convey him to emergency services, ultimately saving his life. The charges he faces for unauthorized entry to the United States seem minimal compared to his imminent death by gunshot wounds. This scene allegorizes the manner in which the United States frames its entire immigration apparatus as bound by law but nonetheless humane, if not humanitarian. *Border Wars* aligns Border Patrol with rescue missions through the Border Patrol Search, Trauma, and Rescue units (BORSTAR) that provide tactical medical services (EMS), combining law enforcement, emergency medical treatment, and search and rescue in one unit.

The show exhibits what Paul Amar describes, in relation to the 2011 revolution in Egypt, as a new era of the security state, in which military intervention occurs under the alibi of humanitarian protection and rescue to form a model of governance based on humanized securitization. Military projects secure the nation and protect cultural patrimony and legacies under threat by outside forces. Security forces ostensibly operate to safeguard human and civil rights rather than, as is the case under the Patriot Act in the United States, sacrificing civil rights for national security.[34] The Border Patrol model of surveillance infuses this humanitarian security ideology into its practices at the border in a deeply contradictory manner. Migrants are rescued by Border Patrol agents from conditions created by CBP policy—prevention through deterrence, enforcement with consequences, and the political and economic consequences of foreign policy in the Americas.

Border Patrol agents extract migrants from circumstances so dire that apprehension and arrest seem desirable, even sought after, deflecting from the larger institutional frame created by immigration policy that makes such conditions so dangerous and untenable. *Border Wars* features a Catholic outreach center in Nogales, Sonora, Mexico, the Centro de Atención al Migrante Deportado / Aid Center for Deported Migrants, run by Rev. Sean Carroll of the Kino Border Initiative (season 3, episode 4). Migrants deported to Nogales often lack basic necessities, making them vulnerable to exploitation by traffickers who offer guided entry to the United States in exchange for drug-mule services. The center attempts to forestall this possibility by providing a safe haven where migrants receive aid in the form of food and shelter before continuing their travels. Migrants are encouraged to return home, with warnings of the dangers of unauthorized entry to the United States. One man describes how he intends to attempt unauthorized crossing of the border as many times as necessary, regardless of legal ramifications, because he has no alternative. The narration ends with a prophetic refrain about the cyclical nature of border security, thus again invoking the trope of Border Patrol agents' overwork, rather than the political and social conditions that cause refugees to flee their home countries.

In *Border Wars*, the depiction of agents' humanitarianism is not limited to the activities of BORSTAR. In one wild chase in the desert, migrants are dispersed by the ominous presence of a Black Hawk helicopter. The helicopter is a technology of surveillance, pursuing the migrant from the sky, while its other, more ominous role is veiled in the narrative. It is often used to intimidate and frighten with aerial spotlights, searchlights, and forward-looking infrared radar (FLIR) with heat-seeking capabilities, along with loudspeakers to leverage and sonically amplify CBP's aerial power.[35] In *Border Wars*, migrants are targets on the ground, described as "bodies" in a group that outnumbers the agents in pursuit, ensuring that many will evade capture. The agents leverage their advantage via their aerial view, guiding agents on the ground when they lose track of the migrants. The view from above is familiar, iconized by the eye of the drone, which is less a part of daily operations for these agents and more symbolic of total surveillance from above, achieved more often by helicopter. The remaining holdout, a quick-moving and evasive man, elicits the ire of agents, who chase him on foot, guided by directions from high above them. During the chase, we are made to identify with the agents' fatigue and frustration and eventual relief when the migrant submits to custody. They do not capture him by force or skill but by luring him in with a bottle of water; the terrain, following the policy of "deterrence," does the work for them, and "humanitarian" aid secures the arrest. These scenes convert perceptions of Border Patrol from an enforcement agency to one of care and protection, serving to individuate and humanize agents and shift attention away from the larger state apparatus. In other cases, Border Patrol agents and their adjuncts, local police, save migrants from the cruelty of traffickers. On *Border Wars*, border agents describe how some of the migrants work for cartels transporting drugs under duress, through threat of violence or manipulation, while others escape gang and cartel violence to seek asylum as refugees in the United States. Migrants are targets of traffickers, shifting attention from their targeting by the US border-surveillance apparatus. Instead, our focus is guided to border agents as objects of surveillance, subject to workplace scrutiny and control and to watchful eyes from the other side of the border.

In borderveillant media, Border Patrol agents are deemed martyrs of a system that puts them at risk in myriad ways. They are vulnerable as objects of potential violence, while they are inculpated by the very system of surveillance that they must enforce. Much of the criticism about *Border Wars* focuses on the security conditions that target migrants and naturalize the militarization of the border. It is part of a number of docuseries, with international spin-offs discussed in chapter 4, about government institutions, more specifically about Border Patrol or police workplace activities and cultures. It puts policing agents under the same surveillance that they enact on migrants. In the episode "Dirty Money," the fifth of season 2 of *Border Wars*, the supervisory officer explains that the increase in personnel creates new vulnerabilities, as traffickers attempt to infiltrate by recruiting naïve or crooked agents. Agents are subject to polygraph tests and internal surveillance through a culture of lateral surveillance, or as one officer remarks, they all "keep an eye" on each other. Collaboration with migrants or laxity in enforcement or execution of procedure is not tolerated. Migrants and traffickers are frustrated in their efforts to "game the system" by studying agents' behavior and timing entry to correspond with the shift of an agent who is deemed a "weak" link. These strategies are prevented with various tactics, such as lane scrambling and random or last-minute assigning of posts. Agents accept this control of their maneuvering with stoic complicity. They are not at liberty to resist or contest this surveillance since they are themselves nodes in a larger network of security. They play out their roles as willing enforcers of borderveillance in a manner that obscures their own subjection to a security regime. Theirs is both a workplace and a symbolic national zone of surveillance. As enforcers of the law, their own freedom is highly circumscribed. They must undergo total internalization of the surveillance practices and procedures that they represent. It is indeed, as the recruitment copy for Border Patrol job opportunities promises, a career with borders but no boundaries.

Privacy Capital

The southern border is defined as a Wild West, a place where the rule of law is suspended in a manner framed in border-security shows and endorsed by audiences. That is, within the generalized state of emergency and state of exception normalized after the events of 9/11, people in the United States are willing to sacrifice the protection of certain rights for the sake of national security. Cultural productions about the borderlands from the vantage of the United States are part of a long and ongoing security and surveillance narrative that continues to frame migrants as subordinate, marginal, abject, and permanently mobile. In the current logic of surveillance culture, they are also stripped of rights, primarily the right to privacy. And within reality TV culture, migrants are only legible as mute or inscrutable criminals, not as "authentic" selves or confessional subjects. Yet, to appear on these shows, subjects must sign releases; otherwise, their faces are blurred, and their images are sufficiently obscured as to be unidentifiable. Yet the conditions under which migrants sign away their privacy rights are problematic, with many impediments to valid and informed consent, including language barriers, the coercive frame of immigration custody, emotional distress, and lack of understanding of the terms of permission.

Within the logic and value system of entertainment-based surveillance cultures, migrants are defined by an abject physicality as moving bodies—they are actually referred to as "bodies" by CBP agents, objectified by the view of the camera. David Lyon deploys Christian Metz's adaptation of the psychoanalytic concept of scopophilia, pleasure in looking, to describe the enjoyment derived from watching without being seen within a surveillance regime. In voyeurism, scopophilia's turn toward the perverse, this pleasure is combined with power over and control of an object; the latter is characterized by a lack of full agency and is typically a female figure, particularly when looking coalesces with anxieties about castration in the psychoanalytic scenario, but this objectness also extends to racialized figures. In the surveillant scene, the exploited object, visible—however indistinctly—but unaware of this fact, is denied the right to privacy and to informed consent, or as Lyon describes it, this voyeurism "reduces the rights of the watched."[36]

In reality TV, the right to privacy is vexed; it is brokered as part of a spectacular display of subjects as "authentic selves" within emotionally wrought stories in shows like *Big Brother* (CBS, 2000–) or *The Bachelor* (ABC, 2002–). Privacy is traded for visibility, as the ultimate and most revered of rights for US citizens. Privacy is brokered for fame. While reality TV stars may have given their consent, those who appear as a consequence of police activity along the border often have not granted consent in a manner that is valid. Undocumented migrants are not in full control of their privacy capital; it is traded on by the producers for audience confidence in the security regime of the United States. The more migrants we see, the better the security system seems. And when we view these same migrants from surveillance cameras or the eye of the drone, we are reflexively engaged in a mediated surveillance regime, one that is as entertaining as it is reassuring.

Border surveillance media demand willing acculturation to a national ideology—one that shifts over time and across regions along the border but remains fundamentally grounded in policies and practices of exclusion. We learn, for example, in *Border Wars*, how to visually sort migrants and identify an "anomaly" in processing vehicles at the border. We look for things that do not fit, contraband objects not worthy of entry. We learn how to identify the coyote, or guide, within a group of immigrants, all of whom are guilty of feigning ignorance of his identity (the show does not feature any female coyotes). The guide is guilty of deception and engineering the entire illegal operation and must be treated and processed separately. In most scenes, the CBP outsmart the coyote, who is identified through his suspicious lack of accoutrements or more readily through recognition as a repeat offender. But the exercise of discovering his "true" identity gives the audience practice in one of the major discourses of the series: discernment of authenticity for purposes of exclusion. There is a kind of do-it-yourself ethos to border patrol drawn from the discourses of the reality television universe. Domestic defense is part of a reassuring moral world with diffuse boundaries in which real and framed events coalesce.

These shows have a pernicious reality effect for their proximity to actual events—they capture actual arrests that are carefully edited and framed to enhance and privilege CBP priorities and apply them to other policing units, from state to local forces, and to acculturate audiences to the militarization of the police. For example, *Law on the Border* is about police work in Nogales, while it is also about the integration of policing agencies of border cities at the territorial limit of the United States. The men on the show all have nicknames that convey their unique skill or character trait that enhances their competence. This recalls a similar gambit on the TV show *The A-Team*, about members of a military command unit who are unjustly accused of crimes and who reconvene in Los Angeles and use their special skills to solve civilian crimes. The "A-Team" configuration was revised in the border film *Extreme Prejudice* (1987), from the first epoch of war-on-drugs media that marked the militarization of the borderlands.[37] These media introduce audiences to the collapse of policing and military units, bringing the technology and ethos of war to the border.

Of all the shows, it is *Border Wars* (2008) that truly brings the war home. It accomplishes this in part by displaying the newest technology of border security, shipped in directly from Iraq and Afghanistan: the MQ9 Predator B drone. The Predator is foregrounded as the ultimate machine for providing the most comprehensive search and location capabilities, particularly within a genre that highlights the entertainment value of the chase within the context of war and its accoutrements.

The split city of Nogales, or Ambos Nogales, in Mexico and Arizona, is depicted as a laboratory of militarized security. On the southern side of the border, migrants prepare to encounter the various impasses that beset them on their journey, along with the technologies for discovering them. The city is divided by a three-mile fence that comes to an end in the desert but is within walking distance of the town on the northern side of the border. An agent describes how interdiction must be immediate, within minutes, or the migrant will become absorbed into the urban infrastructure. Nogales, Arizona, is the occasion to unveil the coordinated efforts of the security apparatus aimed at these migrants. There is a force of agents that patrols the city along with hundreds of ground sensors, infrared cameras mounted on unmarked trucks, mobile generators that charge high-intensity lights, Predator drones, and a command patrol center that monitors all of these technologies directed against migrants as if against enemies of war.[38]

Reese Jones explores the show in relation to cable networks' preoccupation with all things related to "war" and to the banalization of war in everyday life, from a show about warring pastry chefs, *Cupcake Wars*, to the competition to outbid potential buyers at auction in *Storage Wars*. He explores how the "war" of *Border Wars* is similarly hyperbolic in the disjuncture between the events and characters of the show and the aesthetic framing of them. For example, the music, editing, and lead-up to a major pursuit by numerous agents, aided by various technologies, the accoutrements of staging a war, often yields not a fierce enemy threatening the safety and lives of the agents but a group of exhausted and beleaguered migrants risking their well-being for the opportunity for low-wage labor in the United States. Though migrants are framed as enemies of war, the images of their prosaic realities give forceful visual counterarguments to the show's preamble and the rhetoric of the over-wrought voice-over narration. Jones argues that the show plays a crucial role in shaping perceptions of a distant zone, encouraging and corroborating the demand for the intensification of militarized policing.[39]

Surveillance and Resistance

Border Wars conveys the various hindrances and barriers to entering the United States for migrants entering on foot; some are natural, like the river or the harsh desert lands, and the rest are a conglomeration of security technologies and techniques that hinder entry to the more accessible borderland cities. For migrants who evade border security, their itineraries are instances of creative resistance, intervention, reimagining of surveillance, and enacting countersurveillance along the border. Some even redeploy the weaponized environment to their advantage. The manner and possible kinds of resistance are varied. Gary Marx, whose work on police surveillance is foundational to the field, delineates a taxonomy of twelve resistance or neutralization moves including discovering, avoiding, piggy backing, switching,

distorting, blocking, masking, breaking, refusing, explaining and con-
testing, cooperating, and countersurveillance. Each tactic involves
various ways of detecting, subverting, refusing to comply, or avoiding discovery through concealing identity, distorting information, or
breaking the mechanical means of detection.[40] These are all forms of
everyday resistance that, while they do not accrue to an organized
social movement, disrupt the system that controls migrant mobility.
For example, Border Patrol agents in *Border Wars* lament their position
as permanently visible to spotters on the Mexican side. Migrants and
traffickers leverage their higher ground to keep watch on the agents as
they patrol the city; in doing so, they reverse the surveillance regime.
Resistance at the border includes using the natural landscape, taking
cover and concealment, tunneling, and co-opting the vertical power of
the militarized border regime. Through these and other challenges, the
idea of the border as sealed or rigid is defied, and the border is subsequently resignified as flexible and shifting.

Border Patrol agents equipped with night-vision goggles, surveillance aid from above, and surveillance from mobile units on the ground
are foiled by a natural landscape that is redeployed and redefined from
being "weaponized" to serving migrants' advantage. Thick brush provides cover from agents, and the open desert is strategically used to
hinder agents' efforts to capture migrants, who disperse in all directions. Various natural conditions provide cover that foils agents' efforts
at detection. In an episode of *Border Wars* called "Operation Fog Cut-
ter," fog conceals border crossers from agents, while in another episode,
the moon illuminates an otherwise-dark path. The rugged desert offers
means of concealment: contraband can be hidden in deep cuts in the
rock or camouflaged by rock piles in what is called "rocking up."

Migrants challenge and defy the rigidity of the border and US vertical
power through the use of unbounded airspace. In season 3, episode 3,
of *Border Wars*, the ICE agent Kevin Kelly notes that the Nogales corridor is replete with ULAs, or ultralight aircraft, that drop bundles of
contraband across the border, spending only moments across the border
airspace before slipping back into Mexico undetected. The pilot of the
ULA on this episode uses the light of the moon to his advantage to spot
agents on the ground and evade capture. This form of countersurveillance is thematized across independent cultural productions, particu-

larly Alex Rivera's *Sleep Dealer* and his countersurveillance drone project with Angel Nevarez, *LowDrone*—discussed further in chapter 2—and other forms of art that critically expose the violent and invasive gaze of drone vision.[41]

In borderveillant media, migrants are only legible as criminals, either as undocumented migrants or traffickers. There are a number of visual cultural projects that resist and contest this erasure, particularly the Border Film Project, which began in 2007 and arms migrants with cameras to amplify the view of migrants. The visual work of the Border Film Project engages the technology of surveillance from another angle. While migrants document their journeys, vigilantes along the border, whose vantage coincides with images in dominant media, are also armed with cameras to document their surveillance of the border. As a result, the border vigilantes, the Minutemen, assert an individualized gaze, one that is grounded and localized, so that each Minuteman's gaze is peculiar and unique, rather than the policing view of mainstream media. This project aims for more than simple visibility or representation. It reshifts the gaze of surveillance media, unsettles it, moves it from the polarized moral universe of good and bad guys to the more nuanced aesthetic and social concerns of the borderlands. In this visual world, vigilantes and migrants are humanized and rendered as political and social subjects. The three artists, scholars, and activists behind the project—Brett Huneycutt, Victoria Criado, and Rudy Adler—explain the impetus behind their work as seeking common ground between migrants and Minutemen: "Migrants and Minutemen have very different backgrounds, yet they share one profound belief: both sides would agree that they are documenting a situation that should not be happening. U.S. border policy is broken and needs to be fixed."[42]

Rebecca Schreiber argues that the premise of the project to "show both sides" reproduces and endorses the "side" already represented by the Minutemen in their practices of migrant surveillance through camera-equipped drones and night-vision scopes. Given the symbolic power and privileged vantage afforded those who are on the side of law enforcement, the Border Film Project does appear to perpetuate state surveillance. Perhaps there is another archive of the visual record of the borderlands that this project might engage or into which it could intervene. It does, however, reconfigure, somewhat, the dynamics of the surveillant gaze. The Border Film Project, typical of documentary media, has a different valence in a space under permanent surveillance for the purpose of controlling mobility. It turns the sorting gaze of borderveillance media into one that seeks to understand by localizing and particularizing the political agents of the immigration debate. The vigilante perspective, seen from below, is grounded and separated from the vertical power of the border-security regime. While this project arms migrants with cameras, the use of other technologies, particularly cell phones, tells another story about resistance at the border.

The cell phone has potential for insurrectionary uses in the borderlands, depending on how and where it is deployed. A team of researchers—Bryce Newell, Ricardo Gomez, and Verónica Guajardo— traveled to the border at Nogales to get a sense of how migrants use information and communication technologies—cell phones, computers, internet—to get the information they need to make the journey across the border. The researchers found that there is little use of cell phones since traffickers can mine them for phone numbers that become an avenue for extortion and fraud. Indeed, closer to the border, Customs and Border Protection agents use Stingray, a cell-phone tracking device, to locate migrants. For Newell, Gomez, and Guajardo, the lack of a technological intervention or solution to the problem of navigating the border journey is a profound indictment of techno-utopianism, or the idea that "technology will automatically help marginalized populations."[43] Information circulates unmediated, through word of mouth, through stories from return migrants, and through other face-to-face encounters.

Though cell phones are problematic technology during the journey toward the border from the south, they are an important technology of countersurveillance, following the popular use of cell-phone filming of police activity under the "cop watch" movement. Along the border, this idea is replicated through various cell-phone apps including MigraCam, started by the ACLU of Texas, and Quadrant 2 Inc., Notifica, and Cell 411, which capture video that can be sent to friends and relatives by text and email.[44] These apps are particularly useful on the US side of the border, where CBP agents operate with little oversight. There are several instances in which videos posted to YouTube have created public awareness of CBP and ICE abuses.

Figure 1.2. MigraCam app by the ACLU of Texas. (ACLU of Texas, "MigraCam," accessed June 14, 2020, www.aclutx.org)

MigraCam has an additional feature: it includes information about migrants' rights. It is reminiscent of a prototype created by Electronic Disturbance Theatre, the Transborder Immigrant Tool, which guides migrants through the desert to water stations while delivering poetry to users. While MigraCam provides information and countersurveillance for the purpose of protecting migrants, the Transborder Immigrant Tool is a system of care, mapping routes through the desert by way of water sources while sustaining migrants' sense of humanity through aesthetic means. Both resist state control, and the Transborder Immigrant Tool resists state violence of the diminution of migrants' humanity by creating what the contributing artist Ricardo Dominguez describes as "multiple emotional structures that would allow refugees and immigrants crossing the border to feel that they were being cared for and welcomed to the other side by communities, but also, that they are bringing cultural and poetic knowledge to our communities as well."[45]

The Transborder Immigrant Tool and other projects emerged out of the Electronic Disturbance Theater collaboration with b.a.n.g. lab (bits, atoms, neurons, and genes), which began in 2004. Together they created a border art and technology research center at the California Institute for Telecommunications and Information Technology

(CALIT2) to challenge the idea that the San Diego and Tijuana border-lands are a laboratory solely for military research, specifically the Border Research and Technology Center (BRTC) and to develop "gestures that could create conversations about art, social power, and technology in multiple public spaces, as well as critical technology to disturb the border technologies being developed by programs like BRTC."[46] This and other forms of resistance to the surveillant apparatus at the border remind us that the technocracy is neither inevitable nor infallible and that other forms of resistance, through activist revision, take on the surveillant border regime and convert it to powerful research, art, and performance.

"Shoot Now and Ask Questions Later"

The fantasy of complete control of the border through integrated technology that enhances policing was not realized. Instead of a wholesale system, CBP introduced key technologies with particular security objectives, and a culture of border surveillance emerged to support its operations. Reality docuseries about US borders enact the practices of security, which begins with the premise of screening, the collection and processing of data, but accomplishes the greater aim of image capture. These images are collected, collated, and organized into story lines, of which the guiding metanarrative is the unrelenting chase, or the "cat and mouse" story, out of which emerge narratives of deception and transgression, from "imposter" tales to accounts of the increasingly inventive means of transporting contraband.

The Texas Ranger dictum "shoot now and ask questions later" is the refrain of a culture of visually documenting and recording events without limit. Perhaps the future promises, with automatic target recognition, classification, and firing for drone technology, a collapse in the dual meanings and practice of "to shoot." The border-security model, and borderveillance in general, veils the threat of violence within its screening and visual apprehension processes. The threat to life is coupled with a threat of statelessness as the evidentiary criteria for citizenship is rendered ever more arbitrary, particularly when citizenship status is questioned and adjudicated at territorial borders, maritime boundaries, and ports of entry.

Surveillance does not end with biometric screening from the sky or at border checkpoints. Migrants who are suspected of unauthorized entry to the United States are tracked on social media and socially engineered and lured into compromising their private data. Federal policy makes the handing over of cell-phone and social-media data mandatory upon entry to the United States, while drones along the border erode privacy protections more generally.[47] The total system is replaced by this master symbol: the drone. The emblem of this new turn enables complete situational awareness and total intelligence of a scene, providing an omniscient and seemingly omnipotent point of view. The first of such drones, the Predator, deployed along the border supplants and transforms the "cat and mouse" game along the border with the more dramatic and lethal dynamic of predator and prey. It ambitiously promises a future of total surveillance within an integrated system of control that extends from the sky to land and beneath the ground.

2

Drone Futures

Alien versus Predator

The difference between science fiction and science is timing.
—Colonel Christopher B. Carlile, director, UAS Center of
Excellence, Fort Rucker, Alabama

The drones we had allowed us to save lives. They reduced
collateral damage. They gave our soldiers intel, allowing us
to peer into the future on their behalves [sic], predicting
what would occur rather than simply letting it.
—Brett Velicovich, *Drone Warrior*

They see the death penalty coming. They see it coming from
God.
—Jacques Derrida, *The Death Penalty*

A short "three-minute teaser" on the National Geographic (Nat Geo)
website for the show *Border Wars* is titled simply "Predator." In three
minutes, it delivers the entire strategic and technological role of the Predator B drone for Customs and Border Protection. The teaser previews the
series, foregrounding the drone as the ultimate in Border Patrol rein-
forcement and an instrument of expansive data capture. When the agent
on the ground loses the target and requires backup, the drone, operated
from a remote station, is summoned to provide a total informational
map of the scene. Or the hovering robot captures real-time images of
movement on the ground, to which agents are deployed in Black Hawk
helicopters, in all-terrain vehicles, or on foot. The drone is the primary
and organizing node in an integrated, mobile, and highly adaptable
system of border surveillance; or so it is in the theory and ideology of
border-security futures propagated by the CBP and its cultural adjuncts.

The border is the future of national security as much as it is the past of the western lore of the United States. The southern frontier engages both temporalities across diverse narratives and imaginaries about the border and migration, from news stories to reality TV, fictional TV and filmic narratives, and military future maps of drone-enforced security along and beyond US borders. The US-Mexico border has long been a military workshop of technologized control and mass surveillance. Border history is US history, a mythopoetic past of chaotic extremes and racial conflict that is deeply embedded in the cultural unconscious. Along the future border, drones are the new frontier cowboys, imperious, omniscient, and hypermobile. They, to borrow the language of the US CBP 2020 strategic plan, help extend the "zone of security" and "transcend the physical borders of the United States."[1] Paradoxically, they enforce borders as they transgress and defy them.

Drones are part of a plan to "increase situational awareness" and expand mobility for "nimble and flexible deployment" to the "highest risk regions in the border environment," often with great extravagance through blatant disregard for efficiency or cost considerations.[2] The extravagance of drones has various tributaries of meaning in relation to the ongoing low-intensity conflict, or war on drugs and migrants, along the US-Mexico border. The drone, particularly the Predator B, is a sign of excess related to the exaggerated affect of an anxious security state always at the ready for a preemptive strike. It signals the profligacy of Department of Homeland Security spending on a technology that far exceeds the security outcomes at the border.[3] And it is a sign of the surplus of US wars in which the border is the repository of the excess technology and human capital of foreign conflicts. The drone signals the state of permanent war, one that is both domestic and foreign at once.

Drones return from war zones to manage domestic emergencies. While they are part of a surveillance regime in which data is captured, sorted, and used to manage risk, the rationalization in targeting is undermined by the presence of drone operators, making operations fundamentally contingent and negotiated.[4] As a master symbol, the drone hovers alone without any visible sign of its many operators on the ground, concealing its human engineers in a manner that enhances its perceived omnipotence. Abstracted from the world below, it is an emblem of the vertical power of asymmetrical war; along the southern US frontier, it indexes what National Geographic calls the "border wars."

In speculative fictions, military strategic plans, border and immigration policy, Air Force recruitment videos, and Customs and Border Protection future maps, from dystopic to utopic imaginaries, the drone signals a future of complete surveillance, total information awareness, and control of global mobility. The borderlands metonymize the interior and entirety of the nation as a laboratory of security techniques and procedures. Control of the perimeter presages control of the nation. Power and dominion belong to those who manage the mobility of migrant populations through aerial machines and various other technologies. Drones promise omnipotence and clairvoyance by capturing information about threats and enabling forecasting and prediction within a region deemed an abyss of knowledge and the unconscious of the nation. The border drone is the future of security. The future of security is not blockades and barriers but total surveillance and information awareness of and arbitrary control over mobility, along with the power to assert or recognize borders at will. Or as the Republican US senator Kay Bailey Hutchison asserted when drones took flight in Texas in 2010, "We are working hard to make round-the-clock surveillance the standard for all 2,000 miles of the U.S.-Mexico border."[5]

Predator and Prey

Mediations of the borderlands present security as a dynamic of predator in pursuit of prey that terminates in death or defeat of the target. Defeat is retreat or capture, arrest, and deportation of the migrating body. National Geographic's *Border Wars* describes this scenario succinctly. The borderlands are described as a "kind of battleground" where a "high-stakes game of cat and mouse is played out between those who want to cross the border illegally and those whose job it is to stop them" (season 1, episode 1). Drones turn the "cat and mouse" game, described in chapter 1, into a "high-stakes" technologized pursuit of Predator (drone) and "prey." They are part of the opening credits in a montage of the various technologies employed along the border to gain advantage and leverage CBP's goals. The thunderous and highly visible

Black Hawk helicopters represent overt surveillance, while the drones, quiet and unseen, represent covert operations, all of which underscore US omnipotence and omniscience. As proxy border patrol, drones are more capable agents and predators who track and target migrants in a dynamic that might be more aptly called "alien versus predator"—in reference to the blockbuster Hollywood science-fiction film of the same name. Popular cultural accounts of the borderlands corroborate and conspire with US state discourse about the region that poses agents of the law against migrants as invidious or violent bandits and outlaws.

The drone signals a division between hunter and hunted. It is emblematic of predatory techniques and technologies that target vulnerable populations through the militarization of immigration control. Global inequity follows the drone. The division of the world into Global South and Global North is marked by a separation between predators and prey: those who have armed drones and those who do not. This divide is managed, in part, by the US government, apparent in the development of new laser technology capable of eviscerating rogue drones to maintain asymmetry in the field of drone warfare.[6]

Drone surveillance at US borders is not about discovering "patterns of life," as it is when it seeks out alleged terrorists in war zones; but, rather, it anticipates patterns of migration, and more specifically, it seeks to reshape these patterns. Along with the entire security apparatus at the border, drones shepherd migrants to dangerous and inhospitable terrain and expose them to death or injury. Migrants are not simply rerouted, demobilized, and denatured; they are captured as image and information that are fed into an integrated tactical infrastructure. Borderland future fictions reveal the obliterating potential of information or of death by data through future plans for predictive algorithms that automate target recognition, classification, and firing. In fact, the Department of Homeland Security has piloted programs along the US-Mexico border for drones with on-board biometrics for facial recognition or "other biometric at range."[7]

While the current drone technology originated in Israel, it quickly migrated to the United States, and the latter has dominated the market and claims responsibility for setting the ethical terms of use. It is the ultimate sign of US hegemony and imperial overreach, capable of crossing borders at will and without consequence. The deployment of these robots to the US-Mexico borderlands is a logical extension of the militarization of this zone. Drones, also called UAVs (unmanned aerial vehicles) or UCAVs if they are armed (unmanned combat aerial vehicles) and RPAs (remotely piloted aerial vehicles), are piloted remotely from the ground, often very far away from their flight path. Drones are the master symbol of the surveillance apparatus at the border, composed of fixed, mobile, portable, and scalable pieces within a multiagency security regime. They are one of the technologies that the Customs and Border Protection describe as a "force multiplier." Moreover, the US military prefers to use variations of the term "unmanned" rather than "drone" to highlight and forecast a future of complete automation.[8] They signal a shift from the policy of "prevention through deterrence" to that of "enforcement with consequences" through the capability for tracking and targeting and ultimately having the potential to deliver consequences in the manner of their war-zone kin, using the logic of preemption.

The paradigmatic border drone, the Predator B, is empty of features; it has no anthropomorphic elements—though its original name, "Albatross," indicates its animistic origins. The Predator is unarmed, though a 2010 "concept of operations" report by the CBP indicated possibilities for a "payload upgrade" that includes munitions.[9] It is smooth and featureless, neutered, giving it the appearance of blank and anesthetic neutrality. It looks like a plane but one devoid of exposed functional parts. The Predator drone embodies the fantasy of an antiseptic machine without parts, a screen or tabula rasa.

The southwestern-border drone operations began in 2004 as a "pilot study" that was deemed successful and thus extended to the Caribbean, Gulf, and northern border regions. Along the border, UAVs are used to supplement intelligence gathering and increase "situational awareness" for Border Patrol agents. The Department of Homeland Security in 2012 declared that drones along the border would provide "command, control, communication, intelligence, surveillance, and reconnaissance capability to complement crewed aircraft and watercraft and ground interdiction agents."[10] Drones are deemed adjuncts rather than agents of the law; they extract information and enable the tracking of bodies. Their deployment is symbolic, amplifying the image and perception of US power. The Air Force officer David Deptula describes their strategic use: "the real advantage of unmanned aerial systems is that they allow you to project power without projecting vulnerability."[11] This projection of power is abetted in media depictions, locating border surveillance in western lore that draws on an aura and historical era of uncontested US preeminence, particularly in the documentary television shows *Border Wars*, *Border Security: USA*, and *Bordertown: Laredo*.

Drones are part of a sophisticated integration of surveillance technologies that includes watch towers, helicopters, night-vision scopes, radar, and a number of other technologies under development by a conglomerate of border-security companies clustered in the University of Arizona Science and Technology Park, or Tech Park. The US-Mexico border is a security laboratory for the rest of the United States and the world that represents billions of dollars in corporate investment and government contracts.[12] Border reality shows are part of a propaganda machine for these technologies that showcase the advanced state of the art of border security. These productions are signs of the expansion of surveillance culture into everyday life in a manner that supports and justifies the consolidation of the security state. There is a counterarchive of postdrone surveillance story lines that resist or expose the violence of drone futures, including Alex Rivera's *Sleep Dealer* (2008), Ban Lethal Autonomous Weapons' short film *Slaughterbots* (2017), and *Black Mirror*'s episode "Hated in the Nation" (Netflix, aired October 21, 2016). In each of these productions, the drone is a cultural node in a global security complex capable of targeting, classifying, and eviscerating dissident operations.

In the United States, the use of drones expanded as part of overall border defense in the Secure Fence Act of 2006, itself an outcome of the rewriting of border policy in "Operation Blockade / Hold the Line," which began in 1993 and was a template for and precursor of "Operation Gatekeeper" in 1994 and "Operation Rio Grande" in 1997.[13] These policies shifted from apprehension to diversion and deterrence within the logic of preemption, from agents on the ground to mediated surveillance technologies, sensors and drones, and physical barriers.[14] The new strategy, officially described as "prevention through deterrence," shuttles migrants away from urban areas and into more hostile terrain and exposes them to dangerous conditions that often result in death.[15] Since these policies were initiated, migrant deaths have increased dramatically.[16] Migrants are pushed into the hinterland, invisible to urban border populations and mainstream media; their deaths are attributed to the risks associated with the journey, not the risks to which they are exposed by policy. The drone oversees this scenario; it is part of the machinery of the state that determines who may be admitted to the United States and who is barred entry and shepherded farther into the desert to face death or defeat. Though prevention through deterrence was put to rest with the policy of "enforcement with consequences," it established migration corridors that deviate from urban centers and continue to put migrants at risk.

Drones mark a new era in what Timothy Dunn describes as the ideology of the low-intensity warfare along the border that was designed to regulate and shape the flow of migrants, rather than prevent it. Dunn describes development of the militarization of the border region from 1979 to 1992 in the use of military ideology and the entire military apparatus and arsenal within an ongoing warfare that required unprecedented coordination across military and policing units.[17] This era of low-intensity conflict created the conditions for the production of a unique surveillance cultural formation, one that is highly mediated. In 1940, the Immigration and Naturalization Service (INS) was transferred from the Department of Labor to the Department of Justice and took on the character of other agencies under this umbrella, like the FBI, becoming more secretive, deceptive, and propagandistic. Border patrol, by World War II, became a national security issue. After 9/11, the Department of Homeland Security centralized national-security agencies under its aegis, linking domestic and foreign security.

Dunn describes "prevention through deterrence" as marking a major transformation in border policy and practice, one that constitutes the basis of border security and, by extension, national security.[18] Deterrence was a cornerstone principle of national security during the Cold War, which morphed into preemption after September 11, 2001. As a doctrine, aspects of deterrence were rehearsed along the border before it was reworked and deployed as foreign policy. Border policy is moving quickly toward officially enacting the logic of preemption, which it currently deploys in unauthorized rogue attacks or the preemptive strikes of individual CBP agents who, following their Texas Ranger predecessors, shoot first and ask questions later.

The border is deemed a front line and staging ground of the "War on Terror." For "Cato," a former senior counsel at the US Department of Justice, terrorists "weaponize" immigration, targeting the US-Mexico border: "In the end, illegal immigration and terrorism, like water, seek the path of least resistance. The Southwest border, with its vast openness and proximity to transnational crime groups, hostile nation-states, and powerful highways, is the singular approach of a terrorist into America. Illegal entry—once perceived as the least threatening means of terrorist infiltration—now presents the greatest threat in the universe of risks."[19] All forms of immigration are deemed part of the "universe of risks," since, in a specious argument, "immigration, secure borders, and terrorism are linked, not because all immigrants are terrorists, but because nearly all terrorists in the West have been immigrants."[20] In this logic, immigration itself is the risk that demands greater surveillance through more rigidly defined borders, tighter information management, and preemptive control measures.

The Border Patrol strategic plan for the years 2012–2016 adds a new dimension to the logic of preemptive action and "enforcement with consequence" at the border through big data or integrated information regimes. This plan identifies three core pillars—"information, integration, and rapid response"—that mark a rhetorical turn from being "risk-based" toward efforts to "get ahead" through "intelligence driven" tactics. The primary aim to "get ahead," "be predictive and proactive" through information emerges from the policy precursors of "Operation Hold the Line" and "Operation Gatekeeper" within a post-9/11 "threat environment."[21]

The 2020 Border Patrol strategic plan foregrounds preemptive principles while responding to post–Great Recession concerns about economic solvency and stability and expanding the scope and focus of border security to the entire United States. The 2020 plan seeks to protect US trade interests while expanding the territory of the borderlands security plan to areas "outside the U.S. border, at the borders and into interior regions of the country." The "zone of security" permeates all regions in a manner that transcends "the physical border of the United States."[22] Following the shift in security priorities in the former plan, from migration control to risk management, this plan intends to "maximize the use of information and intelligence to analyze risk, prioritize threats, and anticipate emerging trends."[23] The decisive shift to a future-oriented model, through data that enable the anticipation of threats and the mapping of possible threat futures, puts these plans and their ideological orientations into the realm of the speculative. The arc of this speculative logic justifies the preemptive action of aggression. Such is the plan presented in the 2010 Customs and Border Protection report to Congress called *Concept of Operations for CBP's Predator B Unmanned Aircraft System*. This report outlines future and "far term" possibilities for the border drone program; one significant plan to "increase mission effectiveness" is to automate and weaponize drones, enabling them to autonomously seek, identify, and immobilize targets. The report, requested by the Electronic Frontier Foundation under the Freedom of Information Act, was released, highly redacted, for public consumption in 2012. It contains the following section, titled "Payloads," about the future plan for armed drones, that bears quoting at length:

> Mission sensor upgrades could include improving SAR [synthetic-aperture radar] point target resolution to well below one foot, a simultaneous SAR-GMTI/MMTI [ground moving target indication / maritime moving target indicator] mode and advanced ATR/ATC algorithms [automatic target recognition / automatic target classification]. Visual and IR [infrared] band sensors will be updated with new generation arrays. The addition of an Electronic Support Measures suite with specific emitter identification will increase mission effectiveness by enabling the UAS to independently perform the SDCIP [surveillance, detection, classification, identification, prosecution] Identification task. Additional payload upgrades could include expendables or non-lethal weapons designed to immobilize TOIs [targets of interest].[24]

The plan is clear: it includes arming the UAVs to "increase mission effectiveness," which includes not just identifying but firing at targets of interest to "immobilize" them.

The armed UAV in this future projection is presciently dramatized in *Sleep Dealer*, in which a character is targeted as an "aqua-terrorist" for resisting the privatization of water resources. The wages of not just arming but equipping the drone with advanced ATR/ATC (automatic target recognition / automatic target classification) algorithms that target, classify, and obliterate is played out in the cautionary film *Slaughterbots*, uploaded to YouTube on November 12, 2017, by Stuart Russell and Ban Lethal Autonomous Weapons, the activist AI group at the University of California at Berkeley, and funded by the Future of Life Institute (FLI).[25] Indeed, the major difference between prevention and preemption is the main plot point of this short film, in which activists are preemptively murdered through drones acting on the part of unknown and unidentifiable entities.

Brian Massumi neatly delineates the epistemic and ontological difference between prevention and preemption, according them distinct imaginaries and futurities. Prevention operates in a more stable order: threats are known and knowable, and their causes are identified and might be neutralized along a linear causal course. Prevention does not have an internal logic: the means to prevent are contingent on the causes, and as a result, remedies are applied from the outside. For Massumi, "Prevention has no proper object, no operational sphere of its own, and no proprietary logic. It is derivative. It is a *means* toward a given end. Because of this, preventive measures are not self-sustaining. They must be *applied*, by an outside source. They are not an organizing force in their own right. They run on borrowed power."[26] Deterrence moves in where prevention fails. It is a procedure triggered by the urgency and expedience demanded of an emergency. The threat met by deterrence is not emergent; it is fully organized and realized as danger, with a "menacing futurity" that must be met with equally menacing destruction, as mutually assured destruction (MAD). Mutually assured destruction is a "balance of terror" that creates equilibrium in equally developed systems of defense and destruction. This system has an internal logic and energetic balance. "It becomes self-propelling."[27] Thus, an epistemological condition becomes a mode of being, or an ontological condition, and an operative logic. The future effect energizes and provides the causal mechanism in the present. It is singular and monolithic and presupposes equality between opposing forces.

Preemption goes beyond deterrence. It is a strategy deployed when deterrence cannot work because the threat is unknowable and thus cannot be overcome, remediated, or neutralized. The opponent is likewise unknowable, uncertain, and not subject to logical inference. The epistemology of preemption is defined by uncertainty, and the ontology is unspecified, as is the enemy. The only certainty is the surprise attack. The logic of preemption emerges within a permanent condition and atmosphere of threat with an "ontological status of indeterminate potentiality."[28] There exists an imbalance between opposing sides from which asymmetrical warfare emerges, resulting in the "becoming terrorist" of each side. The operative logic of preemption traces the future arc of border policing as an exemplary practice of the security state as "becoming narcoterrorist." The spectacular displays of violence and mayhem attributed to narcotraffickers and cultivated in borderland *narcocultura* is matched by CBP in the deployment of omniscient and omnipresent aerial robots and the spectacle of the multidimensional surveillance apparatus. Drones, though unarmed, are nonetheless spectacular and extravagant displays that are haunted by the specter of past carnage in foreign wars.

Migrants are targeted as enemies of war. They are exposed to death, rendered invisible and silent, denied privacy, and subject to representational slippage into a category of threat occupied by terrorists and drug traffickers. This collapse of boundaries between migrant and terrorist/trafficker emanates from war, particularly in the rhetoric in the War on Drugs as it dovetails with the war against terrorism. The migrant is both criminal, as "illegal," and enemy, as "narcoterrorist." The war was never against "drugs" but against drug-source nations in the Southern Hemisphere and their representatives. Drugs gained an ontology that collapsed with that of their mode of human transport, so that every migrant is treated as a potential carrier of some invasive narcotic strain.

There is a slippage between mediated narcoculture and drug-traffic-related violence along the border. Stories of narcotraffickers are epic and marked by unpredictability, savagery, and cold displays of sadism. Some notable examples in US media are the characters of Francisco Flores, also known as Frankie Flowers, in *Traffic* (2000); the Salamanca cousins in *Breaking Bad* (AMC, 2008–2013); the various traffickers in the *Sicario* franchise (2015, 2018); and more generally traffickers in Mexican *narcocultura* in *cine negro* or *cine fronterizo* and in *narcocorridos* that mythologize drug kingpins as bloodthirsty but heroic renegades. These depictions stand in for and amplify actual events, providing justification for more extreme CBP measures against "narcoterrorists" in drone warfare.

The logic of border warfare, its unifying principles, emanates from US-Mexico borderlands history. In particular, the model of "preemptive manhunting," or what would become "targeted assassinations" of Israeli military strategy, originated in the US involvement with the battles of the Mexican Revolution. These strategies diverge from warfare as composed of battle lines and fronts. General John J. Pershing's military objective was to capture the Mexican revolutionary Pancho Villa, who, in US western and popular cultural lore more generally, is the original "bandit." The Mexican bandit persists in emblematizing lawlessness, immorality, and the disruption of Anglo US culture. The bandit also represents the evasion of law and normative methods of military application of force. The small, mobile groups of revolutionaries formed lithe and flexible units that could readily escape capture. For this reason, Villa remained elusive, and Pershing failed in his objective to capture the revolutionary leader. This failure was instructive for the US military, which adapted its strategies to become as mobile and flexible as the revolutionaries and, later, narcoterrorists in order to launch surprise targeted strikes. Asymmetrical warfare is premised on an imbalance of power, knowledge, and control. This vital workshop of power developed along the border was globalized and then migrated back to the region, before finding its way deeper into the US heartland. George A. Crawford, in a report from the Joint Special Operations University, describes this as "manhunting," in which there is a predator and the preyed on. This strategy of counterinsurgency through robot attacks "deprives the enemy of an enemy," creating a new kind of asymmetrical warfare.[29]

A common refrain in border-security story lines is the idea that moving bodies cannot be positively verified as either migrants or narcotraffickers/terrorists. In *Border Wars*, the Predator B is rolled out as advanced technology, "battle-tested in Iraq and Afghanistan" and "nearly invisible to radar," that can pick up human form on camera from nine miles above the ground but cannot distinguish types of migrants, unlike agents on the scene. The migrants are located through a complex and integrated system of tracking and surveillance. The drone is adjunct to boots on the ground, frontier cowboy types, skilled in tracking and locating "fugitives" through their knowledge of the terrain and typical routes of transit. Each mobile body is preemptively treated as a possible narcoterrorist, often to the disappointment of CBP agents. Or as the narrator of *Border Wars* cynically intones, "This is what securing the border means: using four agents, two jeeps, two ATVs, and one helicopter for approximately four hours to track down three tired and thirsty men who came to this country looking for work" (season 1, episode 1).

Border Wars describes the Predator B as a "silent invisible killing machine" but revises this assertion by noting that "on the border, its job is only to watch and tell agents on the ground what it sees" (season 1, episode 1). Yet, as the "concept of operations" CBP report, cited earlier, asserts, this is possibly a temporary state of affairs, prior to a future munitions "payload upgrade." Border policing and immigration-control prevention through deterrence is more accurately deterrence as a precursor to the preemption of robot warfare. Drones detect emergent threats, but in the logic of preemption, detection is not sufficient as a merely defensive gesture. Defending the border does not protect it; preemption demands offense. Action as offensive brings about the nascent threat, justifying the strike.

As migrants move, they are deterred through exposure to dangers that limit their survival. At the border, deterrence describes how mobility is managed in order to move migrants into ever more precarious circumstances and ultimately, through death, to prevent their entry to the United States. The logic described by Massumi works in reverse or via a different attribution of meaning to each term in a rhetorical gloss. According to the policy language, deterrence precedes prevention, the latter is a sanitized alibi for the former. More plainly, deterrence along the border is death. Prevention encodes the violent process of migrant elimination through death, sickness, or defeat and retreat. Or as Jason Mark, editor in chief of *Sierra*, notes, "The Border Patrol's strategy is calculated homicide disguised as immigration policy."[30]

Good Drone / Bad Drone

Borderland drones are sublime objects invested with the fantasy of a secure and internally coherent entity whose desires for security are readily met, against a reality of the insecurity of open borders.[31] In much of the literature about the ethical considerations of drone use, there is a split between good and bad drones, concisely evoked in the Facebook group

"Good drone / Bad drone," devoted to diverse perspectives on UAVs. This split resonates with Melanie Klein's similar discussion of good/bad objects that either nurture or annihilate.[32] This schema evokes a context of conflict complicit with the war-zone habitat of the drone, while it evokes a moral dilemma. In the psychic developmental arc of the good/bad object, the subject successfully fends off the forces of annihilation to achieve the balance and stability of integration of good with bad. US popular culture neutralizes ambivalence about drones by privileging the entertainment and humanitarian drone over its murderous counterpart. Or if the latter appears, as in the science-fiction B movie *Drone Wars* (2016), the drones are defeated in the assertion of human primacy and intellectual superiority over intelligent machines. The splitting of good humanitarian, entertainment, consumer, and commercial robots from their "bad" deployment as killing machines obviates questions concerning the military origins of this technology. The entire theater of war along the border exposes the false splitting of the drone along affective and moral lines and undermines its assumed neutrality.

For Martin Heidegger, if we regard technology as something "neutral," we remain unaware of the "essence of technology."[33] It is not merely a tool instrumentalized to some end but a "human activity." Technology is the entire system of thinking that generates it and the interconnected objects that compose it: "The manufacture and utilization of equipment, tools, and machines, the manufactured and used things themselves, and the needs and ends that they serve, all belong to what technology is. The whole complex of these contrivances is technology. Technology itself is a contrivance—in Latin, an *instrumentum*."[34] It asserts dominion over human thought, replacing it with practical and mechanized forms of thinking. "The threat to man does not come in the first instance from the potentially lethal machines and apparatus of technology. The actual threat has already afflicted man in his essence. The rule of enframing threatens man with the possibility that it could be denied to him to enter into a more original revealing and hence to experience the call of a more primal truth. Thus where enframing reigns, there is *danger* in the highest sense."[35] Enframing or technological framing signals human subjugation to technology. The idea of a "lethal machine" might allude to war machines and certainly alludes to atomic power. It would not be too far afield to locate the lethal robot as the origin of the end of human thought, thus prophesy-ing the dangers of artificial intelligence. Heidegger warns of the perils of untamed nuclear ambitions: "In what way can we tame and direct the unimaginably vast amounts of atomic energies, and so secure man-kind against the danger that these gigantic energies suddenly—even without military actions—break out somewhere, 'run away' and de-stroy everything?"[36] The anxiety about the nuclear age, like that of the information age, is about the automation of weaponry, that the latter might escape control through a "runaway" mechanism like the culti-vation of the autonomy of intelligence. This is powerfully conveyed in the dystopic science-fiction film *Ex Machina* (2015) and the short film *Slaughterbots*, mentioned earlier—in each, robots gain autonomy and destroy humans.

Technological innovations are so dazzling that they render us un-able to confront them meditatively: "we even marvel at the daring of scientific research, without thinking about it."[37] Heidegger's warning about technology follows logically from his privileging of a particu-larly grounded form of being, emblematized by the peasant rooted to the land who was readily co-opted by a racist ideology under the ban-ner of "blood and soil." Heidegger's personal commitments to Nazism, though short-lived, sully his legacy as a prescient thinker of the various potentials of technology. His student Hannah Arendt took his legacy in another direction in her writing on the origins and operations of totalitarianism.[38]

There is a prophetic tone to Heidegger's writing about technology. He suggests we shape our relation to technology as something adjacent to being, not core to it, lest we become adjuncts of technology and sub-ordinate to it. His essay "Question Concerning Technology," published in 1954, is drawn from his Bremen lectures, delivered in 1949, in which he ponders a complex series of questions about the technological age. This was followed by an address in 1955 about the impact of technol-ogy on forms of meditative thinking. In this discourse on thinking, he prophesies that "the approaching tide of technological revolution in the atomic age could so captivate, bewitch, dazzle, and beguile man that calculative thinking may someday come to be accepted and practiced as *the only way* of thinking." The remedy to this diminution of thought is "releasement toward things" and "openness to mystery."[39] It is this form of human contemplation, of thinking for itself and not for some practical or instrumental end, that is not common practice in models of artificial intelligence and machine learning.

Other Heideggers, Other Futures

The drone future is imagined otherwise in Ricardo Dominguez's short story "Dronologies," which features a science-fiction reworking of Nathaniel Hawthorne's "Dr. Heidegger's Experiment," published in 1837—some fifty years before the other Heidegger was born. In Dominguez's story, the autonomous and armed drone future has come to pass, and these robots are now obsolete. The science-fictional Dr. Heidegger is a "synth-bio" who seeks help in the final stage of his QF-4 experiment to resurrect zombie drones that run "lethal autonomy algorithms exceeding all human capacity" and were put to rest fifty-five years prior. The fictional interlude in the critical text captures the lapsed humanness of the obsolete technology, as Dr. Heidegger reanimates the dead machinery:

> He uncovered the drone node and threw the faded code into the twitching matrix that it contained. At first it lay likely on the surface of the ultrafluid, appearing to imbibe none of its algorithms. Soon, however, a singular change began to be visible; the crushed and dried networks stirred and assumed a deepening tinge of crimson. As if the drone node were reviving from a deathlike slumber, the slender systems and connections of power foliage became green, on, and there was the drone node of more than half a century lost looking as fresh as when GA [General Atomic] had first given it to Dr. Heidegger. It was scarce full blown for some of its delicate red security overrides curled modestly around its moist nano_bios. Within which, two or three switch codes were sparkling.[40]

This work imagines a more complex anthropomorphism of the drone. The drone truly lives not when it is imbued with life and animism but when it is given death, and, in dying, it lives on even beyond death as the undead. In this way, Dominguez's intertext calls on both Heideggers, the scientist of the short story and the philosopher of critical discourse on technology. Dominguez captures, however unwittingly, the future logic of Heidegger's treatise on technology, particularly in the latter's prophecy of the inversion of being and nonbeing accorded human and nonhuman, in which human thought becomes machine-like, calculative, and machines become human in their affective responses and engagements—as does HAL in *2001: A Space Odyssey* or the robots in the film and television series *Westworld* (HBO, 2016–).

Dominguez plays up the ambiguities between human and machine and between fact and fiction. The effect is a confusion of modes that calls into question the conceptual transformation wrought by technology. He, along with fellow artist Alan Paul, staged a drone crash on the University of California at San Diego (UCSD) campus, recalling a similar crash off the coast of San Diego that temporarily shut down the border drone program. These staged events, which took place in close proximity to the US-Mexico border and Tijuana, spectacularly evoke the moral, social, and political issues around drone use along the border—including the announcement of a fake panel discussion on "the topic of drone use on the U.S.-Mexico border" that would feature UCSD faculty and representatives from "U.S. Customs and Border Protection and Homeland Security."[41] The crash was readily interpreted as actual, a perception abetted by the recurrent news media coverage of border drone crashes. In fact, drone operations, including these crashes, are marked by excess, of affect and expenditure, thus exceeding actual security needs.

The Extravagance of Drones, or "Mexico Must Pay"

Drones are an extravagant luxury, an object of consumer and professional desire that promises to enhance human ability, increasing mobility and expanding perception, or "situational awareness" in military jargon. Everyone wants drones. The legal scholar Amanda Porter notes facetiously about the surge in drone sales at the end of 2016, "What do children, adults, photographers, farmers, utilities, agriculture, oil and manufacturing companies, and law enforcement have in common? They all asked for a drone for Christmas."[42]

The drone is a sign of US extravagance, particularly in relation to the Predator drone along the US-Mexico border, a vestige and a totem of the planned disequilibrium of asymmetrical warfare as unilateral warfare.[43] The Predator drone has been targeted as a wasteful expenditure at the border, the squandering of the surplus of empire. A Customs and Border Protection report found that after drone deployment, operational expenses doubled. Drones are deemed excessive, fallible, and unnecessary to Border Patrol operations. David Olive, onetime chief of staff for former US representative Asa Hutchinson (R-AR) likens the use of drones along the border to using a Humvee as a taxi cab: "You know what, it will work, it will do the job, but there are so many other things that will do the job better and cheaper."[44] In 2014, the entire drone fleet was grounded following the mechanical failure of a CBP Predator B drone, raising questions and initiating public debate about the cost-benefit of the drone program.[45]

The idea of drone excess is a useful point of entry for examining the status of these robots in the borderlands imaginary. Excess, for Georges Bataille, is profitless expenditure that disrupts the ordinary, usually as sacrifice and loss. It is "a loss that must be as great as possible in order for that activity to take on its true meaning."[46] Drones are a symbol of power for their utility but are marked much more for their excess as signs of loss of the capital invested in them. Yet power is the "power to lose," and "it is only through loss that glory and honor are linked to wealth."[47] Drone utility is undermined by technological failures and the high cost of maintenance and air time. The destruction of wealth, through these highly capitalized robots, is a form of defiance that asserts the power and hegemony of the North.

In the retributive logic of war, the drone is proof of loss, one that exacts a debt from the enemy state. The cost of warfare along the border produces indebtedness borne by migrants from the Southern Hemisphere. They are defined by the national boundary they cross and are thus totalized and collapsed under the signifier of Mexico. The refrain "Mexico must pay" emanates from this attribution of indebtedness. The object of security, of excessive expenditure, must also bear the burden of its symbolic and actual cost. The idea that Mexico must pay to secure the United States from Mexico is ludicrous and yet falls within the logic of extravagance as waste, loss, and sacrifice that turns the drone into a promissory note. This discourse exploits the association of Mexico with debt, both debt burdens and defaults, that emanates from the Washington Consensus (now ended) and debt imperialism of the World

Bank / IMF variety. This ideology of indebtedness obviates any discussion of the actual debt incurred by the United States through underpayment of migrant Mexican labor, both to the undocumented who pay taxes without receiving the subsequent entitlements and to those who are documented and enter into the bottom of the labor market or are employed below their skill level. In both cases, the United States incurs debt equal to the cost of reproductive labor that is not incurred by the state that receives the benefit of this labor.

Permanent War

Drones calcify the state and cement its borders as emblems of war and violence. Though currently unarmed, they are a key feature of the current reconstituted version of low-intensity border warfare. They supplant outright warfare—at least that was the logic of the Obama administration, which promised to scale back on troop deployments in foreign wars. They are part of a silent or disavowed war that is deemed, as the former secretary of defense Robert Gates cautions, "bloodless, painless, and odorless."[48] This resounds with what Jacques Derrida notes is the logic of the death penalty, which makes "cruelty disappear from the scene." The death penalty is rendered "insensible, anesthetized," in order to "anesthetize both the condemned and the actors and spectators."[49] This anesthetic or anesthesial logic makes death appear painless and rational. Death is a consequence of the reasonable decision of an intelligent sovereign who applies a "medically refined" mode of putting the condemned to death.

The language of the "surgical strike" or "precision strike" in the Obama-era rhetoric of drone killings obviates discussion of the violent cruelty of such strikes.[50] For Derrida, the state enacts divine judgment and punishment through the death penalty, which is the foundational act of the state. Through the death penalty, the "sovereign becomes sovereign" and remains so. The state is founded on this violence, the violence to enforce laws. For Derrida, the death penalty is the key to institutional power: "This is how the essence of sovereign power, as political but first of all theologico-political power, presents itself, represents itself as the right to decree and to execute a death penalty. Or to pardon arbitrarily, sovereignly."[51] The "pardon" is given arbitrarily;

it is doled out as arbitrarily as the death penalty, and both share in the same logic. The possibility of reprieve only enhances the violence that is the condition of the state. The pardon as a reprieve from killing may be likened to the decision to fly unarmed drones along the border, a designated zone of low-intensity conflict. The unarmed drone is nonetheless defined by its potential for a payload upgrade that includes munitions. It remains a machine of war and instrument of violence. It signals violence; it participates in a scene and context of violence and symbolizes the arbitrarily doled-out decree of the death penalty or the pardon.

The penalty of death along the border is not the work of machines; it is embedded in policy. Punishment is doled out as "natural," even "divine," through the tribulations of desert crossing and the trials of terrain and wildlife encounter, or what Jason Mark, as noted earlier, calls the "weaponized wilderness." Migrant deaths are deemed "natural" and accidental through the protected "wild" that represents an entirely different space to the US citizen or resident. Mark notes, "For U.S. citizens, the wild of the United States–Mexico border offers a retreat from the cares of daily life. For the poor coming from the south, the desert wilderness serves as an escape route to a hoped for better life." This space, deemed wild and beautiful and a natural reprieve from urban life, does not readily signify as a weapon. But Mark describes its resignification: "The U.S. Border Patrol has figured out an altogether different function for the big, harsh, beautiful landscape of the borderlands: The terrain has been turned into a lethal weapon."[52] The experience of nature divides along racialized class lines: either it is a reward and reprieve for the irksome labors of the middle class, or it is natural punishment for migrants. The use of the landscape as a primitive weapon may seem to contradict the science-fictional story of a future-oriented and technologized borderlands under total surveillance. Yet nature and machine work together. Drones survey the landscape, allowing the wild to do the work of the death penalty.

Border Futures

In 2012, the retired Air Force major general Michael Kostelnik, head of the office that supervises CBP's use of drones, managed the drone program on the border. He resisted criticism about the drone program as extravagant with a future-oriented retort: "It is not about the things we are doing today. It is about the things we might be able to do."[53] In this manner, the drone program enters the world of science fiction and its speculative imaginaries, alluding to a future of intensified security without acknowledging its potentially violent outcomes. The ultimate co-optation of human endeavor by robot is the usurping of the theo-juridical adjudications of the death penalty. Science fiction imagines this as the consequence of an algorithm that classifies targets to determine who receives the penalty of death and who is pardoned.

Science fiction is an appropriate rubric for exploring the plan and patterns of deployment of drones in the militarized border zone. In an Air Force recruitment video from 2010, the drone, or UAV, is depicted as an advanced technology indistinguishable from that found in enter-tainment culture. The commercial initially appears to be a computer-generated scene from a science-fiction-based video game in which a drone appears on the scene of attack. As the image fades from the warm tobacco hue of the imaginary to the cold blues of reality—an aesthetic contrast notably deployed in the Hollywood border film Traffic—the ta-gline, pasted over the image, declares, "It's not science fiction. It's what we do every day." This commercial is powerfully alluring to a genera-tion that has been acculturated to war through "militainment," or the integration of military strategy and technology with entertainment modes—best exemplified by military-themed video games that prepare and acculturate users to the remote operations particular to UAVs.[54]

The US military is not the only producer of science fiction along the border. In Alex Rivera's Sleep Dealer, the future takes place along the border. The borderlands are a landscape of US colonial and impe-rial ventures, a workshop of globalization and security techniques and technologies, a terrain of ecological degradation, of racial conflict and gender and sexual violence. The border of Sleep Dealer does not erase the past to showcase the future but brings these two temporalities to-gether, foregrounding a vital critique of the fiction of modern notions of linear progress. For Rivera, science fiction projects a vision of the future that alters the view of the present: "Science fiction has a great power and potential to take the world that seems natural and normal around us and make it absurd and unstable."[55] In this future-present, the Global South is associated with hacker culture and DIY hardware, whereas the Global

Figure 2.1. Still from an Air Force recruitment video featuring drone operations. (Posted by Lt. Chuck Smiley, YouTube, October 2, 2010, www.youtube.com /watch?v=TZMl-eYiHmg)

North is aligned with regimes of networked power linking consumer entertainment and global corporations backed by a state security apparatus. The power of the commoner, member of the commons, and migrant workers emerges in historical forms of collectivity and association—that is, not through digital networks. Association and organizing occur on the ground with direct encounter in a manner that contests the future imaginary of the drone security regime.

Rivera, in an interview with Steve Paulson of National Public Radio, calls drones the "meme of our time." He describes drones as the "crystallization of transnational dynamics" and links their mobility to other forms of time and space compression and flexibility, like telepresence and telecommuting. These metaphors are literalized in the subject of the undocumented migrant, who is "here physically but not legally."[56] In the *LowDrone* project, he and his collaborator, Angel Nevarez, graft the lowrider—an icon of Chicano culture—onto the UAV to create a fabulous and culturally specific intervention into the border-surveillance apparatus. In the installation of this project, these artistically rendered objects would fly near the border fence on Mexican terrain and goad the

Border Patrol agents on the other side. In their ostentatious and highly visible appearance, they defy their low-profile and often undetectable drone kin. In another drone installation (*Memorial over General Atomics*), Rivera uses actual bones as parts of the vehicle to incorporate the vestiges of death into the technology of the robot.

In *Sleep Dealer*, drones are aerial gods that exact the punishment of the death penalty without due process. The story line follows a group of interconnected characters drawn together in some cases by their virtual linkages. The main character, Memo, lives in a remote village in Mexico where he hacks into a secure network to spy on government military operations in the United States. In a story inflected with the history of *campesino* struggles in the Americas, the land of Memo's family and its natural resource, water, has been ceded and privatized by corporate powers that sell back the water to the family at astronomical rates. Memo hacks into the government site that puts water activists like his father under surveillance and keeps track of their water holdings in government-protected sites, revealing a clear corporate-military alliance. Memo is targeted as a security risk and subject to a drone strike that incinerates his father, initiating his forced migration north to Tijuana to seek work as a cybracero. Ironically, this and other drone attacks are part of a reality TV show on which Memo's brother is fixated. This scenario recalls events in Central America in the 1980s, when paramilitary attacks protecting landholder interests forced entire populations from their native lands to the north in Mexico and the United States—reflected in the film *El Norte* (1983). And it echoes similar stories of economic exile from debt-addled Mexico during the same era, phobically depicted in Hollywood fare like *The Border* (1982) and *Borderline* (1980).

Drones in *Sleep Dealer* are operated by a single pilot—unlike the actual operation of military UAVs, which employ a team of people. This drone future does not include automation of piloting or targeting. While this may anticipate a different future from that imagined by the US military, it squares with the story line's emphasis on the role and meaning of human agency in the future of the border and the regimes of technologized labor. The pilot reflects the military legacy as employer of marginalized groups, particularly Latinxs. The latter find themselves at war with those who share their heritage and history; such is the case for the entire border-security apparatus, in which Latinx build, manage, and secure the borderlands against racialized invaders from the Global South— including migrants from Mexico, Asia, Africa, the Arab world, and Central and South America. For instance, the entire cast of the docu-reality series about Border Patrol agents *Bordertown: Laredo* (A&E) is Latinx, which reflects the larger reality of Border Patrol personnel. The confrontation of Memo and the Latino drone pilot, Rudy Ramírez (Jacob Vargas), explores this intraracial yet imperial dynamic. Memo and Rudy have commonalities based in shared histories and ethnic heritage that encourage Rudy to explore a past mapped across the space of the border. The actor who plays Rudy, Jacob Vargas, evokes an intertextual history of border media, with a long résumé as a main player in Latinx cinema and Hollywood border film and television—from *Mi Vida Loca* (1993), *My Family / Mi Familia* (1995), and *Traffic* to the border TV show *Kingpin* (NBC, 2003).

Transnational linkages represented by Rudy and other transborder figures are a key component of border media, specifically border cinema; they bring into conversation people in the Global South with people living in the Global North, much like an earlier version of this interlocution in the Mexican-Chicano cinematic collaboration of *Raíces de sangre* (1978). Border media connect those who move between and among borders that are linguistic, ethnic, and geographic. *Sleep Dealer* exposes the integration of the military industrial complex with networked digital cultures that form the basis of global capitalism. It shows how this integration generates new forms of labor.

Memory, as history, is key to excavating these connections. Rudy is compelled to cross the border to find aspects of his own history. The condition of migration is highly mediated and commodified, the source material of a number of ancillary products. For example, on the bus north, Memo meets Luz, a writer who traffics in stories about the marginalized population in the border zone of Tijuana. Memo recounts his tragic story, which Luz promptly turns into a downloadable commodity. The story links Memo to Rudy, the drone pilot who killed Memo's father. The pilot is Luz's first consumer of the Memo line of nonfiction. He buys into Luz's site to assuage his guilt and find a way to make amends. Meanwhile, Luz deepens her intimacy with Memo—whose name is a homonym and root for "memory"—to mine his memory for more marketable stories. Memo's work, including as a cybracero, occurs on the same register for each of his two "bosses"; in both cases, his unconscious is an exploitable resource as a store of both memory and mental labors.

Guest Work as Ghost Work

Curtis Marez finds that migrant labor practices in the California agricultural region might be associated more with a primitive past than the future, much like the small town in Mexico that Memo and his family originate from, which might be associated with predigital culture. Yet from these spaces emerge technologically enhanced transformative practice—for Memo, through his DIY hacking skills—and Marez shows how farmworkers use media and visual practice to interrupt the dominant agribusiness narrative. *Sleep Dealer*, he notes, might be included in the farmworker media archive for its similarity to the farm-to-empire narrative of *Star Wars*. In the latter, Luke Skywalker travels from humble beginnings on his family farm to the center of empire to aid the Rebel Alliance. *Sleep Dealer* evokes repressed aspects of the *Star Wars* mythopoesis to amplify the cultural heritage of labor struggles. Indeed, *Sleep Dealer* is about new forms of labor and association, or as Rivera describes it, it is a "flash forward" on US labor and immigration policy in which borders are closed but cybernetically open as the United States continues to receive all the work without the workers.[57] Though the film draws on the *Star Wars* story line, it is an outgrowth of Rivera's earlier short film, *Why Cybraceros?*, itself a remake of a 1959 promotional film for a short-term-agricultural-labor program, *Why Braceros?* (1997). Rivera's film is a critical retort to Bracero boosterism; it shows how short-term-labor programs dehumanize and instrumentalize workers in the service of capital expansion in the North.

For Marez, the dystopia of *Sleep Dealer* recalls agribusiness fantasies of complete automation and the elimination of workers. The corporate demand for mechanization and technological innovation signals a desire for labor control and discipline as much as it endeavors to eliminate the worker. *Sleep Dealer* imagines a different future for work, one that is not automated but in which the human is a resource for the automation of work. Human labor is not rendered useless or unnecessary; instead, corporations seek new ways of mining labor so that consciousness itself is commandeered and deployed through cybernetic networks. Rivera notes that this idea is about the intensification of alienation for racialized migrant workers: "In *Sleep Dealer* I focus on the impulse toward alienation that is inherent in the system of immigration: wanting work without the physical presence of brown bodies. I use the figure of the robot as a worker without a soul and body as exemplary, glowing, incandescent distillation of this impulse."[58] This alienation, the ceding of consciousness by powerful corporations, targets and impacts racialized populations in a manner congruent with and abetted by the drone strikes featured in the film. Drones epitomize the fear of this Robocop future, particularly one that is not remote controlled but automated and automatic.

The automation of labor means co-opting labor associated with Brown bodies. The science-fictional approach to labor and automation recalls the future world of *Blade Runner* (1982), in which work is performed by replicants, who are defined less racially than by their place in a social order that privileges humans. The human-machine border must be more firmly established, to the elimination or complete subordination of machine to human. The tests to delineate human from replicant recall the Turing test and center around questions related to memory and its attendant emotions. Memories are the most valuable human asset. In *Sleep Dealer*, memory itself is capitalized, accompanied by the capitalization of Brown bodies.

The border is a site of projections both past and present, an archeologically rich and highly mediated zone. The mainstream white-collar anxiety about automation is about the downgrading or elimination of positions. On the border, the twin fears of globalization and subsequent increased migration and computer automation result in a change in labor conditions. For example, in the 1980 film *Borderline*, a couple of buddy-cop Border Patrol agents, once freewheeling cowboys in command of their borderland-territory beat, are threatened with a reduction of their duties to those of a desk job remotely controlling the technologies of border security like sensors and cameras. For people at the bottom of the labor market, work is not ceded to machines; rather, bodies become machines, and labor is produced as machinic operation. The mechanization of the human body in a postglobalized world recalls the women of *Maquilapolis* (2006), who turn their factories' labors into a choreographed performance.

The worker's relation to the machine is key to the Marxian critique of capitalism. Marx describes the experience of automation, in which the body is a "limb" of the machine, subordinated to it and subsequently devalued. The machine carries greater value by virtue of its ontological status as "capital":

> Thus we can see directly here how a particular means of labour is transferred from the worker to capital in the form of the machine and his own labour power devalued as a result of this transposition. Hence we have the struggle of the worker against machinery. What used to be the activity of the living worker has become that of the machine.
>
> Thus the appropriation of his labor by capital is bluntly and brutally presented to the worker: capital assimilates living labor into itself "as though love possessed its body."[59]

In the predigital era, the worker was replaced by or devalued in relation to the machine. In speculative fictions, this relationship is collapsed: the worker is literally the machine, insofar as the machine is capital. The racialized underclasses are capital; their bodies are the origin, and their minds are the medium of capital. For Marx, the relation is one of infusion, "as though love possessed its body," whereas science fiction, from *The Matrix* to *Sleep Dealer*, explores the human as capital whose body and consciousness are mined for their energies. *Sleep Dealer* examines this speculative collapse in terms of the relationship of the United States to the Global South more generally; in addition to workers in Mexico, there is a South Asian call-center worker. *Sleep Dealer* prophesies not simply the automation of work but something more dire, particularly for workers from the Global South. It forecasts the total commandeering of consciousness by digital networks run by corporations and secured by the violent state apparatus. In a literalization of Frantz Fanon's critique of colonialism, consciousness is quite literally colonized and mined as a natural resource.[60]

The story line of *Sleep Dealer* ostensibly grapples with nativism and imperial chauvinism in the demand of work without the worker. However, it is also about the automation of racial capitalism: the demands that migrant workers from the Global South—in conditions very much like undocumented workers living in the United States—expend their life in labor without the entitlements of state belonging that are accorded citizens, including benefits, basic legal protections, labor rights, entitlements from taxation, and due process. And they are subject to the death penalty via drone strike without due process. The film marks a frontier of capitalism in which racialized bodies in their totality, their energies and psychic capacities, are capital for the Global North.

Sleep Dealer is an example of a number of interventions on the border as future zone within science fiction—in stories like *Westworld* that take place in the "Old West" in a manner that thematizes proximity to the southern border and to Mexico and Mexicans or more overtly in the novel *Lunar Braceros*—both discussed further in chapter 5.[61] The borderlands are an archive of border histories and fictions. *Sleep Dealer* presents a different contribution to this archive, one in which border security is embedded in entertainment culture and laboring bodies work not in or for media but *as* media. These bodies broker the fantasy of a borderless world, while the same bodies enact the violence required to secure this world. This story brings forth neglected histories of labor, though for a contemplation of women's histories, we might look to Lourdes Portillo's *Señorita Extraviada* (2001) or the collectively made documentary, mentioned earlier, *Maquilapolis*. In *Sleep Dealer*, the military surveillance associated with the border is part of entertainment media, while it extends to commercial laboring networks. Eventually, Memo and Rudy are able to work together to undermine the security regime protecting neoliberal capitalism. Rudy commandeers a military drone, enabling Memo's village to regain access to the privatized water. The future is dystopic but not foregone.

Along the border, drones function as aerial control and protection of neoliberal capitalism. The drone operates in frontier zones, or what Ian Shaw calls the "borderlands of the planet" at the limits of state sovereignty, with that sovereignty readily violated by the "Predator Empire," or the dronified United States.[62] The drone in the US-Mexico borderlands signals the predator empire within a space of permanent war that is both domestic and international at once. It presages a social order in which privacy is the price of security. The use of drones increased in the early 2000s, prompting a review and subsequent report by the American Civil

Liberties Union (ACLU). This 2011 report exhorts the US government to implement a "system of rules" to protect "Americans' privacy in the coming world of drones."[63] The drone future is one of complete surveillance without any legal encumbrance. The ACLU acknowledges that warrantless aerial surveillance is not categorically prohibited as a result of a series of Supreme Court rulings in the 1980s about the Fourth Amendment. Yet these rulings took place when drone use, because of its prohibitive cost, was limited and required human piloting. Aerial surveillance includes large and small aircraft, humming birds, blimps, and satellites with various technical capabilities, including high-powered zoom, night vision, see-through imaging (capable of seeing through walls, ceilings, or clouds of dust), video analytics that track individuals through facial recognition or other physical characteristics like gait, and swarm video surveillance that creates "distributed video" to view entire cities with no particular identifiable focus, also known as the "Gorgon stare," in which everything is seen.

The ACLU raised prescient concerns about the proliferation of drones in the United States with regard to their impact on the right to privacy. The report notes the likelihood of UAV or drone "mission creep," particularly in law-enforcement use for an ever-widening scope of surveillance through predictive policing, mass tracking, forms of voyeurism on the part of policing agents, discriminatory targeting, and institutional abuse, particularly in attacks on those who challenge norms, along with the possibility of the automation of consequences applied to some of these practices. The report suggests a list of regulatory measures that include restrictions of use through regulation and deployment for specific and clearly defined and delimited objectives relating to criminal wrongdoing, disaster or crisis, or environmental survey. Yet these reformist measures fail to acknowledge the symbolic capacity of the drone, which has become the master symbol of surveillance culture. Nor do they acknowledge the ways that humanitarian uses of the UAV, for disaster or ecological remedy, justify the expansion of the surveillance state.

The security state is symbolized by and legible through the Predator drones deployed along the border. These camera-ready, all-seeing, and covert recording machines, fresh from Middle East war zones, frame the migrant as an enemy of the state. The hypermobile and omniscient drone renders the migrant a permanent target. Though it is not the primary technology of security along the border, the drone is an emblem of surveillance culture, particularly for the way it combines the domains of military, commercial, entertainment, and carceral-policing cultures, while it seems drawn from a science-fiction universe. It indexes a CBP future plan of automatic targeting and immobilizing of targets. Daniel Greene locates the cultural work of the drone in the anthropomorphism of "drone vision," or in "seeing like a drone." When we see what the drone sees, we intuit its desires or see how it operates through the kind of "target-rich" environment that it seeks. Drone vision signals the visual management of the Global South.[64] Along the border, these robots are a technology of sovereignty, an imperial optic that conflates alien, terrorist, enemy combatant, and migrant as equal targets of drone surveillance.

Domestic defense along US borders, of which the US-Mexico border is paradigmatic, extends well beyond continental geographic borders, as it emerges in all points of entry, including airports and seaports. The US geographical border reaches one hundred miles inward beyond its limit, so that border checkpoints appear as far inward as Falfurrias, Texas. The border expands, thickening and calcifying as the surveillance apparatus becomes more buoyant and flexible.

The border is the future of security. The border-security apparatus dovetails with the carceral complex that includes hundreds of detention centers, many privately run, making big business of arresting, detaining, incarcerating, and deporting undocumented migrants.[65] Todd Miller characterizes the system concisely as one energized by extravagant fears: "The border security market is in an 'unprecedented boom period,' to use the words of one recent forecast, and the more danger, real or perceived, the better business has become."[66] The industry is fueled by the production of migrants as the objects of excessive fear. It creates security in the form of assurances of border protection and jobs in the border-patrol industrial complex. In fact, Customs and Border Protection, under the Department of Homeland Security, is the largest federal law-enforcement agency, employing thousands of people under its auspices. When we watch border-security shows like *Border Wars* or *Border Security USA*, we are complicit participants in this system; we identify with and even desire the excesses of empire. We become part of this pervasive security apparatus and its future aspirations, as drones in an expanding hive.

Congress has sought, without success, to arm drones with missiles to strike at drug traffickers seeking to cross the border. Traffickers have instead commandeered drones to their own ends by using small UAVs to deliver contraband across the border. They have shifted the terms of the border drone discussion in a manner that recalibrates the power and dominion of this master symbol. Tony Kingham, editor of the *Border Security Report*, a government-corporate allied publication "for the world's border protection, management and security industry policy-makers and practitioners," notes that small commercial drones are a "real game changer" in the world of transborder migration and smuggling, since they are widely available and "disposable":

> A quick search on google and you can find a long-range cargo drone for less than $3,000, that is capable of carrying two kilograms of drugs up to 20 miles. With a street price of heroin at approximately $100,000 per kilo, it makes the drone a disposable item.
>
> So just taking the capabilities of that one drone, it means that you would have to extend the control or patrol zone around the border, up to 20 miles on either side. That means for the US Canada border 5,525 miles. . . . And of course, that's just for that one drone, there are plenty of others out there with ever increasing capability.[67]

Kingham exhorts a readership of policy makers, technology specialists, and corporate interests to remedy this situation by generating antidrone systems to eviscerate these outlaw drug-smuggling robots. Indeed by 2017, CBP adapted to the new field of operations and began testing a more flexible and less costly fleet of smaller hand-launched drones. The drone future is one in which everyone has drones and the war along the border escalates without end. As the Air Force recruitment video about drone warfare—albeit in other parts of the world—suggests, these speculative musings are not mere prophecy; they are everyday practice.

Critical drone media interrupt this possible future, exposing the violence of the dronified empire and imagining transborder associations that resist the drone future. This future is archeologically layered; while it promises automation, particularly automated target recognition, classification, and firing, it retains the mythos of the Old West and its conflicts. The Predator drones are emblems of border enforcement, extravagant signs of technological progress and efficiency that index cowboyesque border agents on the trail of outlaws. Together, human and machine enforce a regime of surveillance in which a racialized threat is targeted and classified as alien enemy or narcoterrorist. Predator agents and machines ultimately shape and control migration patterns. They shepherd border crossers toward dangerous borderlands desert and mountainous wilderness to face either death or defeat. The border drone hovers over the wildest and most untraversable terrain, where migrants stand little chance of escaping this powerful Predator. Drones are dispatched for various objectives along the border, from migrant observation and targeting to ecological preservation. In each case, border surveillance paradoxically seeks to preserve the wilderness of the borderlands while destroying it.

3

Wild Border

Surveillant Ecologies

The best thing you can do for the environment is to have
control of the border.
—Larry Parkinson, former deputy assistant secretary
for law enforcement and security at the Department of
the Interior

The West of which I speak is but another name for the Wild;
and what I have been preparing to say is, that in the Wildness is the preservation of the World.
—Henry David Thoreau

Open space was the fundamental heritage of America; the
freedom of the wilderness may well be the central purpose
of our national adventure.
—Edward Abbey

The US-Mexico borderlands are geographically and topographically
diverse, traversing twin cities like Ciudad Juárez and El Paso and
Tijuana and San Diego, cutting across wide swaths of inhospitable desert and rugged hills, and demarcated by a river, the Río Bravo del Norte
or the Rio Grande, depending on where you stand. In western lore and
political discourse, the border is a wild and unruly region just beyond
the control of the state, insecure and unsecured from unwanted traffic
in goods and people. It is a region steeped in the history and mythos
of freewheeling cowboys turned gunslingers and Texas Rangers turned
Border Patrol agents who track and ambush resistant Native Americans,
Mexican bandits, narcoterrorists, and undocumented migrants. The
borderlands are a wild place and a hunting ground traversed by hunters

who use their tracking acumen and intuition to trail migrants—keenly dramatized in the Mexican film *El Desierto* (2015).

Before the full-scale militarization of the border that began, in part, with the introduction of Border Patrol in 1924, the southern US border was open and unremarkable. Wildlife like buffalo and bighorn sheep would roam unhindered by barriers, fences, or walls that block free congress and limit access to food and water. For Edward Abbey, the "Thoreau of the American West," according to Larry MacMurtry, "the freedom of the wilderness may well be the central purpose of our national adventure."[1] The free wild is foundational and formative of US national character. The introduction of militarized forms of border security created new impediments to free movement, highlighting fault lines in the diverse meanings of "wild border."

The US-Mexico border emblematizes arbitrary human intervention on a natural ecosystem. It carries the symbolic force of the western frontier before its mythification, particularly its traumatic finitude, and marks the shift from the western to the southern limits of the United States. While the western frontier became "civilized" and settled and incorporated into national identity, the southern borderlands remained wild, a place of limitlessness, of transgression, and, as a contested site, of possible subversion of the hard-won boundaries of the nation. The borderlands inherit the western mythos as a space free of the restrictions and repressions of civilized culture. Civilization, associated with industrialization and urban concentration, destroys the environment and imposes order on nature. The border as wild resonates with the mythic frontier of Wild West freedom and lawlessness in the migration of people and circulation of contraband, while the hardening of the border signals the violence and arbitrariness of setting limits and unsettles the natural ecological balance of borderlands habitats.

The trope of the "wild border" energizes divergent views of the border. On the one hand, the border is uncivilized and out of control, where from a nativist and borderveillant point of view, unwanted visitors invade the homeland as undocumented migrants, bandits, and narco-terrorists. Or the border is not wild enough, and efforts to restore the wilderness are undermined by border-security policies. Since 1983, with the US-Mexico La Paz agreement, there have been transborder efforts to address environmental concerns. This was followed by the Environmental Protection Agency's commitment to further implementation of the Paz agreement with the Border 2012 initiative. However, any environmental regulation might readily be waived, eased, or lifted for military exercises or other national-security activities.[2] The US attorney general has the power to waive environmental laws, particularly the Endangered Species Act and the National Environmental Policy Act, for the purpose of increasing border security. Of particular harm to the borderlands ecology is the ongoing construction of barriers and walls and the disruptive traversal of ecosystems by CBP vehicles. The idea promulgated by Larry Parkinson, former deputy assistant secretary for law enforcement and security at the Department of the Interior, that border security enhances borderland ecology is paradoxical and part of an ideological sleight of hand that justifies further militarization of the region. Moreover, security as wildlife preservation effects a form of ecological nativism that privileges native and indigenous species over invasive species and their symbolic counterparts, migrants. Preservation of the wild requires enclosures, borders, and boundaries separating native from alien invaders.

The various meanings of the wild border and the wilderness are reconciled within a visual borderveillant infrastructure in which ecological conservation is a proxy for migrant policing. The symbolic collapse of immigration and environmental surveillance is apparent in the popular and political mediations of the borderlands in environmental and nature documedia, from the Discovery Channel's *Discovery Presents* episode "Wild Border," the National Geographic series *Border Wars*, and Animal Planet's *Law on the Border* to the Sierra Club's short documentary *Wild versus Wall*. The media about border conservation efforts justify the expansion of visual surveillance, including aerial forms, to control migrants' mobility and to protect wild life. Surveillance is expanded as a means of ecological conservation in a manner that consolidates state mandates to monitor all forms of mobility. Wildlife documentary and other forms of media encode ideas about the "wild border" within the US mythos of the West. In the borderlands wilderness, the enclosure of land for conservation dovetails with efforts to secure the boundaries of the nation. The diverse renderings of "wild" along the border point to an ideological contradiction at the core of US national identity, evinced in the conflict between preserving the cardinal qualities of the national character and impeding aspects of its main prerogative, free movement, for the purpose of national security.

Wild Frontiers

The myth of the Wild West shapes the ethos of the borderlands and their frontier mythos. In this myth, the United States escapes Europe, its restrictions and cultural legacies, to seek out a new order in nature, one that Will Wright describes as premised on various forms of individualism iconized by the cowboy: "According to the individualist theory, this new civil society must emerge from the realm of Nature. Only in uncorrupted Nature—the original State of Nature, the unspoiled wilderness—are individuals truly equal. Nature must generate a free and equal society, and America was seen by early individualists as exactly this realm of Nature. America was the State of Nature, an unspoiled wilderness of freedom and equality."[3] This freedom of the wild state of nature is embodied by the freewheeling and lonesome cowboy who roams the Wild West and whose sense of justice—premised on the rule of White men, private property, and freedom—would establish the basis of a new civil society. The wildness of the American West and Southwest, even as it waned, is the founding myth of the United States, changing only slightly over time as the cowboy transforms into other national icons, from the Texas Ranger to the Border Patrol agent.

The unwilding of the border coincides with the decline of the Old West before the closing of the frontier—declared by the Census Bureau to be closed in 1890, sparking the renowned lecture by Frederick Turner at the 1893 Columbian World's Fair in Chicago, where, incidentally, the myth of the West was in full bloom as simulacra in the same venue in Buffalo Bill Cody's "Wild West" show. The Wild West evoked in the show and in its subsequent representations elicits nostalgia for an era before industrialization and the predominance of urban centers in public and political life.[4] The wild frontier as a place where the buffalo roam was tokenized in the buffalo nickel from 1913 to 1938, turning the West into the currency of the nation. The buffalo nickel captures the fantasy of the frontier as a space of unrestricted movement, as free-flowing as money, emblematized by its animal inhabitants, which represent the full promise of the land.

When the frontier closed, the Wild West became an idea and an aspiration, a horizon of possibility displaced onto other wildernesses, other frontiers. This notion kindled the desire for wilderness exploration that found its apogee and great expression in Jack London's *Call of the Wild*, published in 1903. Preservation of "wild" America required access to preindustrial preserves through the imperial adventures of travel to the Global South. This is exemplified in the adventures of Theodore Roosevelt, who, fresh from his exploits in Cuba and the Philippines, traveled to Africa in search of wild game to import. Roosevelt in the wilderness became a capital venture. Wilderness exploration accrued various kinds of capital, particularly as an object of academic study that finds its contemporary equivalent in conservationism and ecology. The appearance of Roosevelt on the scene marks the rise of the wilderness idea as a cinematic event of national proportions. The filmmaker William N. Selig sought to accompany Roosevelt but was refused and so resorted to reproductions of the hunt in his studio. As the actual hunt hit the news, Selig's cinematic simulation was released in theaters under the title *Hunting Big Game in Africa*, becoming an immediate hit.[5] This ironic scenario was in keeping with Roosevelt's habit of encouraging replicas. When the frontier closed and the Wild West was in decline, he proposed its simulation as a model of rugged adventurism to guide future American aspirations.[6]

The ideas of the Wild West and wilderness are entangled as they intersect with discourses that delimit national identity through an exclusionary and nativist logic. There is a conceptual affinity between the "wild" of the borderlands and the wilderness idea traceable to Ralph Waldo Emerson, Henry David Thoreau, John Muir, Aldo Leopold, and Edward Abbey. For these writers and thinkers, the wild is a place of refuge that must be preserved and protected against interlopers. It is sacred, a place of solace, solitude, communion with nature, and retreat that enables meditation and reflection. The US spirit of independence and self-reliance emanates from the use and appreciation of the wilderness.

Ideas about the wilderness shape its use. The various notions about the wild were formalized in the Wilderness Act of 1964, based largely on Aldo Leopold's 1963 report on the state of nature in the United States. The legislation defines wilderness in the following manner:

A wilderness, in contrast with those areas where man and his works dominate the landscape, is hereby recognized as an area where the earth and its community of life are untrammeled by man, *where man himself is a visitor who does not remain.* An area of wilderness is further defined to mean in this Act an area of undeveloped Federal land retaining its primeval character and influence, without permanent improvements or human habitation, which is protected and managed so as to preserve its natural conditions and which (1) generally appears to have been affected primarily by the forces of nature, with the imprint of man's work substantially unnoticeable; (2) has outstanding opportunities for solitude or a primitive and unconfined type of recreation; (3) has at least five thousand acres of land or is of sufficient size as to make practicable its preservation and use in an unimpaired condition; and (4) may also contain ecological, geological, or other features of scientific, educational, scenic, or historical value.[7]

Much of protected land designated by the Wilderness Act is located in the West, and a large part of these lands abut or are part of the borderlands of the United States and neighboring territories. In these spaces, "man [*sic*]" is transient, a visitor "who does not remain." The space is rife with metaphoric potential as a highly regulated, bounded, and delimited area, resonant with ideas about nationhood and species purity and preservation. Moreover, "man" is modern, a settler colonial, rather than integral to the natural scene; *he* is defined as a mobile nuisance. In the borderland nature preserves, this sense carries over to migrant populations, particularly in a post–1965 Immigration and Naturalization Act era and its logic of hemispheric exclusion; by subjecting Mexicans to quotas, it denies the history and practice of free cross-border circulation for commercial, cultural, educational, kinship, and labor purposes. For the historian William Cronon, the notion of wilderness as marked by human absence defines the human as an interloper fundamentally beyond and outside nature. The "wild" is discursively produced in contrast and in tension with the human.[8] The "interloper" on nature represents human intervention of various kinds as visitor aliens to the natural scene and as mobile or migrant populations who do not belong there.

Roderick Nash intensified the wilderness debate during a key moment in the historical arc of wilderness preservation. He completed his dissertation the year the Wilderness Act was signed into law, and his work explored the concept of wilderness as a chaotic and frightening unknown. Much like the obscurities associated with the borderlands, the wilderness is a chasm into which US fears are projected and contained, captured in the figurative meanings of it as "any place in which a person feels stripped of guidance, lost, and perplexed."[9] Nash argues that the "wild" is a concept created to mark the distinction of human from animal, along with the characterization of nature as beyond human control or manipulation. Wilderness is not neutral; rather, "civilization created wilderness." This marked a new era of walls and barriers in which nature is physically divided between domestic and wild: "Until there were domesticated animals it was impossible to distinguish them from wild ones. Until there were fenced fields and walled cities 'wilderness' had no meaning. Everything was simply habitat, which man shared with other creatures."[10] The creation of boundaries, walls, and divisions is inextricable from the designation of wild.

The 1964 Wilderness Act does not assert an absolute or final characterization of the wilderness. Instead, Nash describes it as a state of mind whose definition is subjective and often nebulous, although he does settle on a meaning based on a continuum of experience and a wide "spectrum of environments" that "puts a premium on variations of intensity rather than absolutes."[11] Nash replicates the early manufacture of nature in amplifying the definitional shift from the unruliness of the untrammeled wild to the instrumentalized wilderness underpinning the National Park System as a necessary and salubrious reprieve from the enervations of the developed world. The shifting valences of "wilderness" are useful for tracing how the concept works in conjunction with other ideas that are foundational to the national character, namely, the frontier and the borderlands.

In the third edition to Nash's foundational wilderness tome, *Wilderness and the American Mind*, he adds an alternate perspective to the culture of wilderness from the point of view of the original inhabitants of the place he calls America—referring to the United States, though the entire continent falls under this designation. He cites "Chief Standing Bear of the Ogalala Sioux" in reference to nineteenth-century contact with settler colonialists.[12] The Anglo-American western incursion invented the West as a wild place in terms of both natural ecology and the absence of social and political institutions. For Native Americans, the "Wild West" is an invention and describes a place that is simply home rather than alien or wild. In *Indian Wisdom*, published in 1933, Chief Luther Standing Bear writes,

> We did not think of the great open plains, the beautiful rolling hills and the winding streams with tangled growth as "wild." Only to the white man was nature a "wilderness" and only to him was the land "infested" with "wild" animals and "savage" people. To us it was tame. Earth was bountiful and we were surrounded with the blessings of the Great Mystery. Not until the hairy man from the east came and with brutal frenzy heaped injustices upon us and the families we loved was it "wild" for us. When the very animals of the forest began fleeing from his approach, then it was that for us the "Wild West" began.[13]

For the Sioux, there was no "frontier" or "wilderness" or space feared as "beyond their control."[14] Yet for the settler colonialist, the wilderness, like the frontier, shares symbolic resonance with the borderlands as places of the unconscious in which the natural and the wild exist beyond culture and control. This legacy is embedded in the very term "wild," which derives from early Teutonic and Norse languages with an etymological root in "will" and its tributaries of meaning in willful, uncontrollable, and unruly.[15] The wild border is "out of control" in a manner resonant with anti-immigration rhetoric, thus requiring the enclosure of protection and external control in the form of surveillance.

The US wilderness idea was created by and in the image and fantasy of renowned Anglo-American men like John Muir, Theodore Roosevelt, Ralph Waldo Emerson, Aldo Leopold, and Sigurd Olson, among many others writing in the tradition established by these influential male figures. Their work underwrites a masculinist and individualist conception of the wild that is foundational for the state project of land protection known as the National Park Service. Making the wild wild again, restoring the mythic promise of the frontier, in part, means restoring animals to their habitats. In the United States, the "wild" is circumscribed and enclosed by policy and politics, much of which emerges from the National Park Service, a bureau of the Department of the Interior established by Congress in 1916.

The Wildlife division of the National Park Service was created after a major wildlife survey in the summer of 1929. Part of this assessment included determining the boundaries of "wild" through scientific and historical discourse, formally defined in the first wildlife study published in 1933, which was also the first statement of the National Park Service's policies on natural-resource management. While the authors of the study held public use as a defining value, they proposed novel solutions to the paradox of the national parks as borderlands of endogenous human and natural worlds. To mitigate the degradation of human intervention, the authors proposed an expansion of the boundaries of parks to accommodate the mobility of wildlife for seasonal migration. In a paradoxical metaphor, given the popular association of borders with barriers against external intrusions, the biologists described inflexible borders as akin to a "house with two sides left open."[16] That is, a house missing walls does not protect its inhabitants, just as park boundaries are a protective limit beyond which animals are vulnerable: within the park, they are protected, and beyond it, mere game. The metaphor captures, in part, the imperial and expansionist logic animating National Park Service policy. The enlargement of parks' geographical boundaries is not proposed for direct capitalist extraction, though it does expand the reservoir of leisure spaces for the American public. The sense of boundedness, of containment and enclosure, points to the discursive engineering of the space of the wild, or what the authors of this definitive National Park Service study describe as the absence of an "original" "wild-life picture."[17] They note a key point of reference in the origination of wildness, however, in the "period between the arrival of the first Whites and the entrenchment of civilization," disregarding Native presence as having any major ecological impact and thus associating the era prior to White settlement with pristine conditions.[18] This unreconstructed idea of the wild, its historical and geographic boundaries, links indigenous wildlife and peoples as congruent if not indistinguishable. And the acknowledgment of a lack of any originary wildness exposes the ideological narrative of the National Park Service as one that is both expansionist and self-perpetuating.

The National Park Service must strike a balance between conservation and public use; the latter includes consideration of the economic benefit of tourism to local communities. As the spaces for wildlife protection expand, the pressure to allow public access intensifies, particularly for the leisure pursuits of hunting, camping, and boating. The value of the park or refuge derives from the maintenance of its character as wild, partly through park boundary protection. Francis Massé and Elizabeth Lunstrum describe this as "accumulation through securitization," in which conservation of natural resources is enacted through the logic of security. For example, the effort to create tourism-related wildlife enclosures for rhinos in the Greater Lebombo Conservancy in the Mozambican borderlands expands the Conservancy's commercial value and security mandate against the external intervention of poachers.[19] As wildlife frontiers expand, so do the commercial opportunities related to tourism.

Another vector of capital expansion through the amplification of national parks is via media, particularly nature shows, documentaries, and related work. The *Discovery Presents* episode "Wild Border," about a binational wildlife park, is drawn from the ideological field of the national parks narrative and traverses the geographical border between the United States and Mexico as well as the ideological border between nature and culture. This episode is part of a special series of programming on the Discovery Channel that covers a wide range of topics related to science, technology, and nature. Like much of the channel's programming, this show frames the natural world with anthropomorphizing narratives about survival, competition, and individual success in a manner that recalls plotlines of reality TV competition shows. It is part of the *Discovery Presents* series programming, which goes in depth about particular topics, although it could also be drawn from Discovery's series *Wild Discovery* from 1995, which is closer in kin to the wildlife documentary genre. The 2015 episode reflects aspects of this previous series but places the newer one in the context of the political conditions of the contested space of the borderlands.

"Wild Border" resonates with competing channels' borderlands shows, particularly Nat Geo's *Border Wars* and Animal Planet's *Law on the Border*, that expose the workings of national security along the border region. "Wild Border" shifts the subject to animals, at times privileging nonhuman beings as central to a natural order while asserting the primacy of humans in their power to restore this lost order. This story delineates various modes of subjectivity along a hierarchy and arc of animism to humanism. It is about wildlife along the border in a manner that exposes the ideological leanings of border tales in Nat Geo and Animal Planet, at times granting animals more agency and entitlement to the land, sometimes in a manner that obviates human-rights issues related to migrant travel. The show is part of a genre of wildlife visual cultures, from photography to documentary films, that seek allegorical insight into aspects of the human animal. John Berger notes in his essay about looking at animals that we are drawn to the animal world, to its wild state, as a nostalgic reminder of the premodern, also the precolonial, and as the dramatization of subjectivity at its limits. When the animal we gaze on returns the gaze, we have been seen, existing in a manner above and beyond the life before us. Seeing wildlife or watching wildlife is to witness the demise of the wild commemorated in the zoo, images of wild animals, toys, and domestic pets; thus, wild animals are commodified and objectified for consumption. Animals become spectacle in various ways, particularly in animation through the Disney industry and in wildlife films. The presence of animals in the reproduction of their likeness is the sign of their disappearance and reemergence as metaphor.[20] Akira Mizuta Lippit describes this cinematic embodiment and representation of animacies, through "animation," as a "gesture of mourning" for the demise of wildlife.[21]

Wildlife filmmaking constitutes a genre characterized by the adaptation of animal behavior to human logic, both anthropomorphic and zoomorphic, in which the animal world elucidates aspects of the human. In borderlands wildlife media, the border is both geographical and symbolic, where nations meet and an allegorical zone of the contact and conflict between human and animal. The wildlife genre offers both sensational entertainment and a lesson in natural history and biology, as, for Cynthia Chris, a "prism through which we can examine investments in dominant ideologies of humanity and animality, nature and culture, sex, and race."[22] As a genre, it is moored in a past that draws on imperialist displays of ethnographic panoramas and dioramas and public zoological parks. Yet it is also self-referential. Derek Bousé notes that wildlife films, while based in actual events, are part of a formulaic genre with its own codes and conventions. These films tend to follow a formula of "successive predator-prey interactions," a convention established by a cornerstone of the genre, *Mutual of Omaha's Wild Kingdom* (NBC, 1963–

1971), and a trope that, explored in earlier chapters, is grafted onto border security and migrant dynamics.[23] This premise forms the ideological link to wildlife media about the borderlands. Moreover, the narrative structure of these films, bolstered by cinematic technique and technology, follows the arc of Hollywood film and TV media storytelling, which is energized by suspense, conflict, and resolution. This narrative arc coincides with the hunt and predator-prey dynamic and the natural cycles attributed to the struggle for survival in the wild. Moreover, wildlife films are premised on the relative laxity of ethical and legal codes around privacy, informed consent, exploitation, and misrepresentation.[24] This ethical gloss pervades the entire wildlife scene in these borderland documentaries, in which the diminution of rights is allegorically applied to colonial subjects, animal and human, in the border zone.

"Wild Border" appeals to a US-American desire for the Wild West and natural limitlessness as an escape from interdiction by invoking animal disregard for boundaries. The narrator prefaces the series with this sentiment: "The US-Mexico border. We drew this imaginary line in the sand, but animals don't see it. Monitored and fenced, buzzing with commerce and contraband. Wild creatures still break the rules." The male narrator speaks with a slight southwestern drawl in the laconic and prosaic manner of a cowboy of western lore. He draws on the poetic ambiguity of "wild creatures," which teases the ontotheological boundary between animal and human, between animals who do not "see" the border and those human animals who cause the border to "buzz with contraband." The narration explains the aim of a binational effort to restore ecological balance to the borderlands: "Now, separated only by the Rio Grande, scientists, both Mexican and American, are working to remake this borderland in its original image, a place of legend and song, where native animals roamed free." The site of this work is a national park, one of many wildlife preserves and national parks along the border designated by the Wilderness Act. These areas are protected against degradation by human activity, defined mostly as cross-border mobility, in order to preserve the natural "wilderness" or the "wildness" of the borderlands.

Borderlands wilderness protection comes into direct conflict with borderlands security, though "Wild Border" indicates this conflict indirectly, through analogy and metaphor. The Department of

Homeland Security, in 2003, through its Directorate of Border and Transportation Security, is charged with security and surveillance of US borders. This entitles the agency to violate the Wilderness Act and traverse protected areas with all manner of vehicle and technology.[25] Migrants likewise compromise protected lands, partly as a result of the Border Patrol strategy of "prevention through deterrence" that shuttles migrants to these areas. Yet it is migrants, not the border-security apparatus and its policies, that are targeted as a highly charged category of being invasive to the nation and its primordial and emblematic lands.

The first encounter in "Wild Border" begins in a manner that is ambiguous, to tease anthropomorphic meaning from its animal scene. "In remote West Texas, four hundred yards from the Mexico border, an ambush is under way. The target is a two-hundred-pound desperado, and he'll do anything to escape." Two men dressed in fatigues and carrying assault rifles communicate covertly over radio as they gun down the "two-hundred-pound desperado." They are "hunting down one of America's most invasive species . . . wild hogs." Until the appearance of the wild hog, the language and the framing of the scene are typical of those linked to tracking migrants in similar terrain on Animal Planet's *Law on the Border* and Nat Geo's *Border Wars*. The men are part of the West Texas Tactical Hog Hunting team. One of them claims that the boars are "predators" that will eat anything. The narrator intones that these hogs "run roughshod over the dream of a more natural borderland." In this *Animal Farm*–like allegory, the boars are "invasive" "tusky beasts" that are not "native Texans" but Eurasian boars brought in for hunting in the 1930s and "released into the wild." The era is significant. It coincides with the period of heightened immigrant phobia and massive roundups and deportation of Mexicans. As invasive intruders, wild boars allegorize contemporary challenges to the border-security apparatus, since they "keep getting smarter" by adapting to the hunt; they are described in a manner that echoes *Border Wars* narration about migrant adaptation to and outwitting of borderveillance regimes. Hunters must likewise adapt their technologies to outmaneuver the boars. This requires setting up trail cameras, tracking patterns of life, and adapting their rifles and scopes in much the same way that the Border Patrol units have adjusted to their "prey." The boars are indifferent to the national politic and care nothing for "lines in the sand," as they make their daily migrations from the United States ("by day they're Americans") into Mexico ("at night they slip into Mexico").

"Wild Border" explains that not all animals are equally deserving of protection or preservation. Some are, as we know from the allegorical morality of the show, unwanted and invasive. Some do not belong. The irksome and unwelcome visitors are an "invasive species" that must be eliminated to secure the natural wildness of the land and restore the balance of the ecosystem. The animal outsiders tacitly align with other invaders: humans, as undocumented migrants, who likewise are inculpated for their deleterious impact on the delicate borderlands ecosystem. Native animals are victims of invaders. Heroic individuals, scientists acting as high-tech shepherds, intervene to restore balance on behalf of the victims of the invasive animals. The boars do the metaphoric work of humans. They embody the biggest threat to the environment: consumption. According to the boar hunters, they are voracious and indiscriminate, tapping out resources for other animals, even preying on privileged borderlands species. These Asian boars are a racialized life form; they summon meaning associated with all things foreign, along with the various tributaries of meaning associated with pigs in US popular and literary culture—specifically, the political and devious pigs of *Animal Farm* and the endearing and savvy Babe of *Babe*, among others from children's tales such as *Charlotte's Web* and *Winnie the Pooh*. Pigs are either adorably timid and domesticated or smart and controlling, even, as in *Animal Farm*, indiscernible from humans in their propensity to fascism—no doubt an origin of the epithet "fascist pig." They are caught in a signifying split between good and bad, the kind of split associated with typologies of inclusion and exclusion within nativist discourses, in which the privileging of the "good" justifies the expulsion or elimination of the "bad." This bifurcation is evident in popular cultural depictions of outcast populations, particularly migrants, most apparent in border westerns of the Reaganite 1980s, in which the good female migrant represents US values and the bad male migrant represents the disruption of those values.[26]

Boars along the border are deserving of their fate of being tracked, trapped, hunted, and killed. They are part of an ecological hierarchy that pits native and wild borderland species against foreign invaders, linking those on the bottom of this animal hierarchy with "foreign" or alien species—notably the Asian boar, framed in a manner that evokes resonances of Yellow Peril discourses and that harks back to the era when Chinese migrants were major targets of Border Patrol.

Wild Boar and Sheep Pig

The popular fascination with pigs as adorable domestic pets followed the publication of the children's book *The Sheep Pig* (1983; published as *Babe the Gallant Pig* in the United States), by Dick King Smith, which in turn followed the 1975 publication of the groundbreaking animal-rights "bible" *Animal Liberation*, by Peter Singer. The latter was reprinted in second edition in 1990, the same year that the Universal Declaration of Animal Rights was made public. These and other transformations across the popular cultural landscape enabled the film version of Smith's children's book to become a cultural landmark. The Australian-American production of *Babe* (1995) earned numerous accolades and inspired audiences to consider animals as capable of suffering and having emotional lives and attachments as beings of conscience endowed with consciousness. *Babe* resonated with people familiar with the social world of animals created in George Orwell's *Animal Farm*, while emptying the story of parable. Singer adds to the cultural status of pigs, which he praises as highly intelligent. He highlights the cruelty of considering them to be mere food and finds them more worthy of the literary acclaim bestowed on them by Orwell: "Of all the animals commonly eaten in the Western world, the pig is without doubt the most intelligent. The natural intelligence of a pig is comparable and perhaps even superior to that of a dog; it is possible to rear pigs as companions to human beings and train them to respond to simple commands much as a dog would. When George Orwell put pigs in charge in *Animal Farm* his choice was defensible on scientific as well as literary grounds."[27] As in Orwell's tale, the animals on the farm in *Babe* are not just proxies for humans but anthropomorphized embodiments of animal life. The film achieved through pathos what Singer proposed through logical argument.

Pigs are at the fulcrum of the ideas and attitudes about animal rights. Singer begins his work with a resounding affirmation of the philosopher Jeremy Bentham's inquiry in defense of animal rights, "Can they suffer?"[28] This question is part of a series of inquiries that seek to delimit human from animal along the axes of consciousness, temporality, language, logic, dexterity, and memory. For Martin Heidegger, it is the hand, origin of writing and *techné*, that distinguishes human from animal.[29] Bentham casts aside these questions to pose the more fundamental premise on which rights rest, that of suffering. Jacques Derrida likewise takes up the long-standing question of animal agency in much the same manner, most notably in *The Animal That Therefore I Am*, based on a series of lectures delivered in 1997. He argues that it is only in relation to animals that humans emerge into being. The idea of a homogeneous and totalizable category of the animal is erroneous since it casts out the human animal from its definition.

The strict delineation of human from animal, in the division and divisiveness of such typologies, is the source of totalitarianism and other extremes in *Animal Farm*. Orwell's parable begins and ends with the machinations of the pigs on the farm, who, being endowed with superior intelligence, become leaders. The pigs create a theory of "animalism," with seven commandments created in opposition to human characteristics and abilities:

1. Whatever goes upon two legs is an enemy.
2. Whatever goes upon four legs, or has wings, is a friend.
3. No animal shall wear clothes.
4. No animal shall sleep in a bed.
5. No animal shall drink alcohol.
6. No animal shall kill any other animal.
7. All animals are equal.[30]

The pigs soon violate these commandments, and the boundary between human and animal dissolves. Much of the literary criticism of *Animal Farm* explores the parable and allegorical dimension of the text in relation to Soviet forms of communism and conflicts among the people in state leadership. However, the novel might be taken literally as part of its multilayered and overdetermined topos of meaning. It gives voice to the animal community within an interspecies hierarchy. The "animalism" of *Animal Farm* privileges animals as morally superior to humans, but this is merely a gambit toward allegory. The characters gain fleeting visibility for the cause of animal rights before the story line lapses into a full-scale anthropomorphic allegory in which animals merely reflect and embody human politics. The list of commandments reflects in part the philosophical interrogation of that which decides the difference between species. Derrida begins his reflections with a version of commandment 3, that animals shall not wear clothing. Part memoir, his lecture "The Animal That Therefore I Am" begins with his naked self-reflection as seen through the fixed gaze of a cat peering at him as he steps into the shower, a scene inflected with John Berger's musings about gazing on animals. Derrida catches himself in an experience of shame for being seen in this way, "for being as naked as a beast."[31] It is this shame for the failures of modesty that marks the human, since animals are unselfconsciously naked, without the sense of propriety to cover one's sex, or "without consciousness of good and evil."[32] Yet this human-animal dynamic cannot be abstracted from the social context imbued by language. Carla Freccero notes that Derrida's cat is female but he refers to it variously, in colloquial French, as "le chat" and "la chatte"—in French, all cats are generally referred to in the neutral masculine or unmarked gender as "le chat," but the reasons for this slippage are likewise gendered. Gender enters the scene obliquely through the mediations of translation.[33] Gender is a technology of anthropomorphism in which modesty is construed across gender difference.

Clothing and dressing oneself are proper to humans, a practice begun perhaps in fear of being indistinguishable from animals. Napoleon, the pig ruler in *Animal Farm*, marks his transformation to totalitarian rule when he and the other pigs walk on two legs and don the clothing of their overthrown human masters, until the two become interchangeable. In the eyes of the "lower animals" outside the circle of power, gazing in on the human-pig junta in the farmhouse, they are one and the same: "The creatures outside looked from pig to man, and from man to pig, and from pig to man again; but already it was impossible to say which was which."[34] The cultural history of pigs as human proxies and vice versa does not begin with *Animal Farm*, but Orwell's novel is perhaps the most enduring and significant text on the subject, originating the idea of pigs representing the very worst of human character: cruelty, duplicity, and gluttony. In other literary archives, pigs also stand in for people at the very bottom of the labor market: the working class.

The guttural sound indicating disapproval, the grunt, is so called for its association with the sound emanating from pigs and forms the root of "disgruntled." Following this linguistic tributary, the "grunt" is someone who performs grunt work or hard physical or low-level unskilled work. This meaning dates back to Samuel Johnson's dictionary, in which swine are associated with the working classes, since they are "remarkable for stupidity and nastiness," a sentiment affirmed by Edmund Burke in his concise description of the working class as the "swinish multitude."[35] Mark Neocleous explores the cultural roots for the association of pigs with the working class to promulgate a dimension of his multifaceted study of the enemy, one aspect of which is emblematized by the disgruntled employee as an icon of class unrest. The pig signals the unruly and insurrectionary mob and a threat to a stable social order, even a threat to democracy as the specter of communism.[36]

The swinish grunt aligns with the disgruntled employee as a potential class warrior rising up against the ruling class. The pig is at the nexus of conflicting and opposing values, a perfect embodiment of the border ecology. Neocleous notes, fortuitously, the role of the pig as a border crosser who straddles "the line between the domestic and the wild, the rural and the urban, order and disorder, liberty and confinement."[37] As a border figure, it is no coincidence that the pig figures prominently in the border imaginary or that the anthropologist Jason De León, in his book *The Land of Open Graves: Living and Dying on the Migrant Trail*, chooses the pig as a bodily proxy for the migrant in the desert to determine the duration of the process of decomposition. He details the killing of the pigs dressed as migrants, along with the process of bodily degradation in the desert. The experiment lays bare the postmortem suffering and the ecological erasure of migrants' deceased bodies. In the process of killing the pigs, we experience a gruesome violence, devastation, and endure the meaning of the desert as an open grave. Some critics ponder if more death is justified to explore the process of death and decay. For Joseph Nevins, De León's lurid description of the prolonged and blood-drenched killing of the pigs is horrific and "contributes nothing of significance to the project, other than (unintentionally) raising questions about research ethics."[38] Others find the lurid to be a means of subversion of the status of racialized migrants in the mainstream imaginary. In a dialogue about mediated forms of fear and loathing of Latinxs, between Frederick Aldama and William Nericcio, the latter notes that the images and descriptions of the pig carcasses are designed to disturb and disrupt and might be deployed against the architects of the very state policies that weaponized the desert. Aldama agrees that the "simulation" or reconstruction "wakes people to the murderous results of the massive increase in high-tech weaponizing of the border."[39] He likens it to Alejandro González Iñárritu's virtual-reality installation *Carne y Arena* (2017), in which participants occupy the place of migrants, thus "turning the tables" on Latinx threat narratives and putting the subsequent horror and violence squarely in the world and psyche of the viewer.

The pigs in De León's experiment and in the mediated stories of border ecology are migrant proxies deemed alien invaders of the wild environment. The borderlands privilege the wild of both the Old West and the wilderness against deracinated types. What makes deracinated animals particularly odious is their outsize gluttony, deemed dangerous to the environment and native species. In fact, the narrator of "Wild Border" characterizes native species as victims of the boars, famished and beset in their search for food. They are oppressed by the unfair conditions along the border of boar dominion, in which the free-ranging boars roam at the expense of other poor creatures. The Asian invaders, evocative of communism applied undemocratically, graft a skewed social order onto the desert landscape. The scientists are the real heroes responsible for restoring ecological balance through interventions designed to promote species equity.

The nostalgia for primitive America and efforts to restore regions destroyed by human intervention are a paradoxical anthropocentrism. They are based on the power of humans to determine the fate of the land for nonhumans and other organisms in a manner that mimes colonial control of resources and the imperial legacies of the hierarchy of species. The colonial dynamic, even within this transformation of the human relationship to nature, privileges nature against the most vulnerable humans struggling for survival. Much of the environmental discourse of which "Wild Border" is a part partakes in the orthodoxies of mainstream environmentalism and the preservation of some pure version of wilderness as a form of imperialist nostalgia. The idea of a prelapsarian borderlands disavows the colonial dynamic apparent at the wild border.

The ecological drama at the border is framed in terms of the ideological primacy of the wild within the romance of the Wild West. In the reshuffling of all of these terms and histories, it is the scientist as the lone ranger who struggles against uncontrollable forces and hostile terrain to bring justice to the border.

Scenes of Nativist Conservation

Along the border, environmental stewardship concerns encode migrant phobia with the idea, expressed by Larry Parkinson, former deputy assistant secretary for law enforcement and security at the Department of the Interior, that "the best thing you can do for the environment is to have control of the border."[40] This sentiment is woven through with nostalgia for the Old West, or in the language of the narrator of "Wild Border," the cross-border collaborations are intent on "bringing back the Old West," which means "driving out invasives." The narrator adds that "scientists, both Mexican and American, are working to remake this borderland in its original image, a place of legend and song, where native animals roamed free." There is continual reference in "Wild Border" to the past and to "turning back the clock," at the same time that the past of the Old West is designated as the future aspiration of the borderlands. The most evocative scene of conservation in "Wild Border" is the "alien abduction" of bighorn sheep for its conjuring of other images of pursuit and capture along the border executed from the sky.

The effort to restore sheep to the free range and then secure their migratory routes can only be achieved "from above." Sheep are pursued by helicopter and trapped and lifted by nets, with the goal to "capture, not kill," the "target." The language of the sheep hunt from the sky is militaristic, resonant with the language of the border drone's aim of capturing and not killing. The military tone and terminology and the images that accompany the narration conjure other scenes of aerial pursuit. The sheep are in panicked flight from the helicopter in a visceral image of hunt or "abduction," in the language of the narrator. They are examined, blood is extracted for testing, their elevated temperatures from "capture-related stress" are reduced with cold water, and they are tagged and collared for release into any number of wilderness areas along the border. These radio tags, used to make animals legible for human purposes,

Figure 3.1. A high-tech cowboy rounds up radio collars. ("Wild Border,"
Discovery Presents, season 1, episode 19, 2015)

evoke Cold War–era surveillance tools and mark the intersection of
wildlife management and military surveillance technologies.[41]

Another scene aligns sheep with migrants, and scientists as the inter-
vening force of human institutions to shape patterns of migration. The
sheep, though a protected species, are proxies for migrating populations,
highlighting the power of the shepherds to deploy technology to reshape
the borderlands. The graduate research assistant Thomas S. Janke, in his
work for the Borderlands Research Institute at Sul Ross State University,
is introduced as a "high-tech shepherd." He searches for signals from
the radio collars on bighorn to track their migratory patterns. He hikes
in conditions of excessive heat and dry, rocky, and hilly terrain, remark-
ing that in his two years of this work, he has yet to come across "any
visitors." "Wild Border" does not evoke or reference any migrating humans, except in this offhand remark by Janke. Migrants are only apparent through metaphor and allegory. The high-tech shepherd describes a
wildlife corridor that "knows no borders." According to Janke, one sheep
crossed into Mexico for Cinco de Mayo and returned after a couple of
days, because "it just liked to party." The major difference between the
migrating sheep and the high-tech shepherd is evinced in their moral
regard for the law. The shepherd will not cross into Mexico to retrieve

lost collars just feet away from him because it is against the law. Big Bend National Park, where he works, is entirely within the United States and part of the national park system. The other side is the Mexican wilderness. The sheep roam both sides of the border. One possible site of the release of sheep after they are round up and tagged is near Coahuila, a state associated with drug traffickers and trafficking in the North and an area that evokes a different meaning of wild, particularly with reference to the idea of the "wild" or "wilderness" from the point of view of the Global South.

The Mexican "wilderness," though coterminous with that of the United States, has a different history and significance to the central state to the south. One main contemporary difference is the cooperation of major corporations in the protection of wildlife. In this case, a Mexican corporation, Cemex, funds the area called Cemex del Carmen within the Maderas del Carmen protected area. This refuge, according to one of the Mexican scientists interviewed on "Wild Border," is one of the last "wild" (*silvestre*) places in North America for its isolation and diversity of species. In Mexico, the northern borderlands are a distant and rugged terrain of inhospitable desert and marauding Natives permanently at war ("permanentemente en guerra") and barbaric ("bárbaros").[42] Hernán Cortés deceptively mythologized this desert terrain as a place replete with natural wealth and precious stones to, unsuccessfully, encourage settlement. As S. Enrique Rajchenberg and Catherine Héau-Lambert note, "for the elites of central Mexico the northern borderland was not a place to go, but one to be kept at a distance" (para las élites del centro de México, el septentrión no era un lugar al que convenía dirigirse, sino mantenerlo a distancia).[43]

The Mexican attitude toward the frontier is in contrast to that of the United States, particularly in nostalgia for the era prior to the closing of the frontier that emblematized the US spirit of adventure into the "wild." Rajchenberg and Héau-Lambert note that this is a longstanding attitude that derives from the colonial era: "According to central Mexico, the immense north was a frontier, not in the Turnerian sense, but in the sense that it was a place from which it was best to maintain distance for its incredible danger. This was not a new idea but one with a colonial legacy." (Desde el México central, el inmenso norte era la frontera, no en el sentido turneriano, sino en el de un lugar que convenía mantener a distancia por su altísima peligrosidad. No era nueva esta concepción, sino una de las herencias coloniales.)[44] The idea that this region is dangerous and untraversable alienated it from the central government and rendered it vulnerable to expropriation by the United States, a result of the war of 1846–1848 that ended in the Treaty of Guadalupe Hidalgo. After the closing of the US frontier, it reopened as symbol and myth, as a place of opportunity and adventure. The myth of the frontier signified differently across cultures. Mexico's lack of esteem for its borderlands enabled various forces to cede this symbolic ground. While central Mexico disdained its northern arid and rugged landscape, this unpopulated region was a screen for US fantasies of wilderness exploits in a region unsullied by the forces of civilization. The interior of Mexico was deemed a place of vibrancy and flourishing, with a fecund landscape and the promises of civilized culture. On the contrary, the northern regions were stigmatized and derided as "torrid and dry regions of rapacious plunder and death" (la rapiña de despojos y la muerte; tórrido y seco). Central and southern Mexico were "full of color and replete with pleasant fauna . . . and symbolized by the hummingbird and flowers" (lleno de colores y de una fauna risueña . . . y simbolizados con el colibrí y las flores).[45] During the early days of the republic, its borderlands inhabitants were alienated from central Mexico, referred to by their locality rather than their nationality.

The different values associated with the borderlands are replicated in the early history of each region, between US borderlands scholars and those studying the northern frontier of Mexico. The Spanish borderlands are marked in part through their institutional formations, particularly the mission and the presidio as defensive bulwarks against Native American hostilities. In contrast to the "rugged individualism" of the US frontier, Mexico's was marked by limits to mobility and self-determination. Spanish absolutism was pervasive and limited the possibilities for self-government.[46] In contemporary depictions of the borderlands, the northern Mexican region is not identified with national identity but is alien to it and remote from its political centers. In the United States, the border is at the crux of national self-regard and often instrumentalized for a story about security and economic and political fortitude.

However, the noted Mexican historian Silvio Zavala argues that there is some continuity between the two frontiers. He finds that aspects of

Turner's thesis about the symbolic character of the frontier applies to the Mexican North, where climate and geography demand a "certain temper and energy."[47] The struggle to survive in rugged conditions demands a pioneering industriousness, much like Turner's frontiers people. Zavala notes that the isolation of the frontier made it suitable for the cultivation of despots who might operate beyond state control. Nonetheless, from the view of central government, this land remained distant, remote, and excluded from a vision and image of Mexican national character.

The frontier, the region at the extreme geographical edge of the nation, is a place defined by law, either in the wild abandon of laws or as a place that tests the limits of the law. The historian Walter Prescott Webb, infamous for his lionizing book on the Texas Rangers, which glosses the genocide of Mexicans and native Tejanos, writes of the frontier and the borderlands in the early part of the twentieth century. In *The Great Plains*, he explores how the pioneers, as they moved west, had to reinvent social dynamics and structures of power, since the laws of the East did not extend to the new environment. In both cases, the borderlands are a frontier zone beyond the law where policing and surveillant infrastructure emerged differently in response to different imagined threats and dangers. The geographical border is a site where law and policing converge for the restriction and control of mobility, along with the inversion of due process in the anticipation and expectation of threat—all migrants are deemed guilty and subject to the legacies of "shoot first," by camera surveillance or historically by Texas Ranger firepower, and "ask questions later." All aspects of the borderlands are managed by surveillant techniques and technologies. The interplay of environmental security with border security amplifies the demand for transparency and control, even as the latter is at cross-purposes with the former, even as the security infrastructure at the border degrades the delicate ecosystem it traverses.

Renegade Roads

The environmental crisis created by the degradation of the fragile desert ecosystem is a consequence of the border policy of deterrence. By closing urban routes in developed areas, this policy forces deviation to undeveloped areas that are subsequently ruined by traffic of migrants and their pursuers. Migrants are inculpated for the environmental crisis that is a consequence of policy that denatures and dehumanizes migrants while instrumentalizing them to force a change on nature and create public sentiment supporting the construction of more barriers and sources of environmental degradation.

The Sierra Club produced a short video, *Wild versus Wall*, that promotes an idea of the "wild" that enhances the division and opposition of security and migrant rights within the discourse of environmental conservation. Its Borderlands Campaign was part of an effort to raise national awareness about ecological degradation at the border. The documentary dramatizes an advocacy strategy developed by Michael McCloskey, a former executive director of the Sierra Club, aimed at finding the most persuasive ways of achieving clearly established aims by identifying and addressing "decision makers."[48] The Sierra Club targets the Department of Homeland Security in an effort to retain the "vital and wild places" "under assault" by a border policy that "can operate above the law" to build walls "at any cost." The Sierra Club supports a national-security agenda with "rational border policies" that allow people "on the ground" to gain "operational control" of the border, rather than "symbolic mandates" to build walls.

The short documentary redefines the borderlands as a biological place rather than a political space.[49] The river is typically characterized in US accounts as a "natural" boundary between nations, as it was described in the 1848 Treaty of Guadalupe Hidalgo. Instead, it is a political marker and unnatural division. In *Wild versus Wall*, Scott Nicol of No Border Wall Coalition describes the river as linking various habitats and connecting them in ways that defy artificial boundaries between nations. US border policy promulgates walls, roads, and outposts as keys to defending the nation by halting human traffic, but various activists, environmentalists, and biologists affirm that barriers only hinder people; they do not stop human traffic, but they do stop animal movement and interrupt the ecological system and create irreversible damage. According to the Texas director of the Nature Conservancy, Laura Huffman, "The fence is the very definition of habitat fragmentation, the very definition of what inhibits free movement of wildlife within its natural habitat."[50] Moreover, the towers, low-flying helicopters, and roads in remote areas disrupt sensitive ecosystems, and lights used to expose migrant traffic

Figure 3.2. Frog stymied by border wall in *Wild versus Wall*. (Sierra Club, *Wild versus Wall*, Vimeo, 2010, www.sierraclub.org/borderlands/wild-versus-wall)

impact nocturnal animal cycles and disrupt animals' alimentary habits and migration patterns.

The documentary intends to publicize the environmental concerns about the border wall with a very specific activist outcome: to have audiences act to get their representatives to repeal section 102 of the 2005 Real ID Act, which grants power to waive local and state environmental laws for border-security purposes. This activist turn requires audiences to trade anxieties about border security for concern about animal and ecological welfare. The latter is effectively presented through numerous images of small creatures stopped in their path, seemingly mystified and stymied by the appearance of a human-made barrier. In one evocative scene, a diminutive frog is cornered by the wall, confused and immobilized, in a heart-wrenching display of the violence of border security to animal life.

For Rachel Shellabarger, Markus Nils Peterson, and Erin Sills, in their ethnography of humanitarian and conservation workers, border security functions as a "commodity," purchased with tax revenue, that veils the conditions and relations of its production. These two groups represent key nodes of ethical debate about the impact of border security, while they also index different paradigms along a human-animal continuum. Humanitarian workers are at times at odds with conservationists in their efforts to provide aid that contributes to the erosion of fragile ecosystems. For example, providing food and water to migrants may result in refuse that harms animals and degrades the desert ecosystem. Both of these groups are at odds with a militarized border-security system that overrides environmental concerns and targets migrants as enemy aliens within a border paradigm of relentless war. In Shellabarger, Peterson, and Sills's study, land-management personnel describe Border Patrol agents and vehicles as having the greatest ecological impact on the region, far outweighing the impact of individual or group migrant transit, most often as foot traffic.[51] These two groups view their work as integrated; while humanitarian efforts are not primary to the conservationist view, in general, conservationists express a moral view that balances responsibility for the welfare of migrants and that of the ecosystem. They do not express legal or politically guided concerns that privilege ecosystems over migrants; rather, they identify border-security policies as the moral culprit. Environmental groups, including the Sierra Club, tend to target border security within a realist political frame; that is, they are more concerned about the border in its current state, in which border security is a necessary evil, rather than imagining a future in which border security is replaced by transnational interdependence or other forms of collaboration and cooperation.

Call of the Wild

"Wild Border" ultimately defends open migration in a manner that continues its anthropomorphic trend: "A more open border stands to benefit people and wildlife, like the Mexican bears that found their way north to start a family of Texans or the big cats that will only survive if they can breed on both sides of the border." This sentiment is premised on wildness as a form of imperial nostalgia for things as they were before colonial extraction, a state of intact human and animal habitats. Moreover, the mythos of the wild frontier evokes what Leo Marx calls the "feeling for nature," or an inchoate desire for a preindustrialized state. This sensibility accounts for the persistence of the western genre and pastoral tales:

> Nowhere is the ill-defined feeling for "nature" more influential than in the realm of imaginative expression. There can be little doubt that it affects

the nation's taste in serious literature, reinforcing the legitimate respect enjoyed by such writers as Mark Twain, Ernest Hemingway, and Robert Frost. But on the lower plane of our collective fantasy life the power of this sentiment is even more obvious. The mass media cater to a mawkish taste for retreat into the primitive or rural felicity exemplified by TV westerns and Norman Rockwell magazine covers. Perhaps the most convincing testimony to the continuing appeal of the bucolic is supplied by advertising copywriters; a favorite strategy, validated by marketing research, assumes that Americans are most likely to buy the cigarettes, beer, and automobiles they can associate with a rustic setting.[52]

Nature provides scenes of escape from the dehumanizing forces of culture. Within this cult of nature, human and animal skills—intuition, sensing, tracking, feeling—take precedence over technological or machine interventions. And the ecological and moral distinction between native species and alien invaders shapes the public mood about immigration and border policy.

The borderlands are zones of contrasts and conflicts, in both aesthetic and political senses, across which the machines of the security regime suddenly appear to disrupt the wild. This contradiction intensifies the imagined conflicts at the border between the Global North and South and between Border Patrol agents and migrants. In these media about wildlife at the border, both senses of the wild border—as the domain of freedom for animal and human and as a wild space beyond the control of the state—coalesce at the expense of vulnerable populations at the border. Borders and limits or outskirts are places of violence for migrants, who are imperiled by the intensification of surveillant policing, resulting in racial profiling and the creation of an exceptional space marked by the lifting of the legal entitlements to due process. The surveillance regime at the border arbitrarily determines the boundaries of protected life; it renders migrants disposable, whose deaths go unnoticed and unpunished, while expanding enclosures for wildlife protection. The US wild cannot be extracted from its mythic imperial history, where freedom and mobility belong to White men and their proxies.

4

Imperial Border Optics

Close your eyes and point to any landmass on a world map, and your finger will probably find a country that is building up its borders in some way with Washington's assistance.
—Todd Miller, *Empire of Borders*

While borders are understood as lines demarcating territory, an analysis of border imperialism interrogates the modes and networks of governance that determine how bodies will be included within the nation-state, and how territory will be controlled within and in conjunction with the dictates of global empire and transnational capitalism.
—Harsha Walia, *Undoing Border Imperialism*

The critique of the security order will only become intelligible when the founding dogmas of the new information order's hegemonic project are challenged: unilateral governance of the Network, the logic of private appropriation of patrimonialization of information, science and knowledge by the dominant entities of the global economy, the exclusive power of market actors to define technical norms.
—Armand Mattelart, *The Globalization of Surveillance*

At the 2019 gathering of border-security experts at the World Border Security Congress, the deputy director of Operations Support of US Customs and Border Protection, Renée Yengibaryan, using examples from the US-Mexico frontier, spoke about border control in a manner that had resounding impact on the rest of the congress proceedings. She noted that while it might seem propitious and insightful to identify trends in security breaches, it is actually a consequence of an ongoing pattern of failure. Rather than a happy accrual of intelligence, the identification of a trend should, she opined, elicit a less positive affect, that of embarrassment ("You should be embarrassed"). A pattern is a sign that border security has failed to be sufficiently predictive of risk. Instead of anticipating threats, agents are rendered defensive and responsive, acting against a past of ignorance and violated security and not in accordance with an intelligent and preemptive future plan. Other speakers, disavowing any possible grounds for embarrassment, referenced this emphasis on anticipating risk over responding to threats as an important strategic position, albeit one that is not new but has been the basis of US national- and border-security policy since September 11, 2001, when all security protocol shifted to the anticipation of unknown futures.[1]

Embarrassment is a dangerous feeling capable of eliciting extravagant reactions. In the border-security context, it signals the affective response to a pattern of failure that constitutes a trend. The moralizing exhortation "you should be embarrassed" exposes the emotional landscape of security in the anxious demand to know everything beforehand, to exhaustively assess, understand, and anticipate risk. Moralizing affect is capable of shaping the tone of public discourse. In this context, presented by an agent of US Customs and Border Protection, it has the persuasive effect of soft power, one that subtends the coercive force of US economic and military preeminence. The mandate of global border security is only partly enforced by moral feelings and attitudes; there are other factors guiding compliance and the coordination of technologies and their mediations. Yet affect foregrounds the role of the humane and human agent as the prime mover of operations through the force of will, feelings, and desire. The human agent guides the engineering vision and cardinal feelings of the entire apparatus, and US CBP assumes the allegorical helm of the global security regime.

Kelly Gates argues that US homeland security is already global; it is not imagined as a local or national institution but a set of reproducible and globalized procedures as the fulfillment of a security-centric form of neoliberal capitalism, enacted under the alibi of international cooperation. She notes the various institutions that shape this international security ideology under the umbrella of the Department of Homeland Security.[2] Indeed, the United States is the founding member and maintains a directive role in global peace-keeping and economic-security agencies, such as the United Nations, the International Monetary Fund, and the World Bank. Moreover, there are a number of international border security and regulation agencies that are part of the United Nations and function in a US border-imperializing capacity. The United States is also the guiding member of an agreement with the United Kingdom and members of the latter's Commonwealth, known as the Five Eyes, in what constitutes an expanded forcefield and fulcrum of imperial command. The US government shapes aspects of the global security mood within this nexus, creating a standard against which no country would or should fall short. This idea of falling short or behind informs the tagline of the International Civil Aviation Organization (ICAO) of the United Nations, the entity responsible for setting global civil aviation safety and security standards; the tagline asserts that in security issues and surveillance capacity, there will be "no country left behind."[3]

This chapter explores how state and entertainment entities shape flows of soft power animating global border-security discourses and practices. The US-Mexico border is a laboratory for border control that functions as an originary and originating site within a wider matrix of power that proliferates across other ports of entry, particularly international airports. I explore mediated tributaries of an Anglo-centric and US-driven circuit of power and allegiance that is promoted and disseminated through cultural means and is apparent across the international docuseries boom in border-security TV shows that underscore the global industrial and state collaboration to standardize border-security practices, technologies, and political processes. This global border-security imaginary accomplishes similar aims in the creation and implementation of imperial norms of border security, enacted and dramatized by human agents through their affective guidance, tutelage, moral judgment, and willed determinations.

The United States maintains a leading role in the border-security network represented by the long-standing international intelligence alliance, noted earlier, known as the Five Eyes, comprising the United Kingdom, the United States, New Zealand, Canada, and Australia. Though the United States is a key driver in global security, it is joined by members of the Five Eyes in the production of a worldwide border matrix that delivers its procedures, operations, and plotlines through various forms, particularly through the global circulation of entertainment culture through popular TV shows about border security. The global border optic is a mediated space where security operations constitute entertaining story lines in which the various technologies, infrastructure, and affective ideoscapes of global border security commingle. These global TV series constitute the entertainment arm of border security across the Five Eyes alliance.

The cultural productions of border security, global borderveillant media, provide the answer to the question posed by the United Kingdom's Border Force command within the Home Office: "How do we export the border?"[4] These TV programs show how border-security operations work in coordination not through explicit means but through the visual and tropic complicity between cultural productions and political discourses. They starkly reveal a clear and defined split between the Global North, represented in part by the Five Eyes, and the Global South. The former polices the latter, creating and instituting the standards and ideals that the rest of the world must emulate and endeavor to attain. The culture of border security generated by members of this formal intelligence alliance evinces shared preoccupations about known dangers, unlawful entry, and the traffic in contraband, as well as unknown or unpredictable risks that impact border practices and subsequently shape global security discourses.

The Five Eyes security protocol for various kinds of international traffic and movement is evident across the border spaces of international airports. The supranational and liminal site of the airport is a common space of action that links borders of the Global North. As a border zone, the airport is a space of governmentality and a laboratory for testing laws while asserting cultural norms and the legal boundaries on immigration. The airport is the key symbolic venue for the petty sovereign who makes decisions about entry to or exclusion from the nation. It is a major locus of the surveillance apparatus and site for the dissemination and wider deployment of technologies and techniques to the general population. Airport security practices partake in cultural norms as they overlap with the legal regime of immigration. Peter Adey describes them as "gateways that differentiate" and sort, drawing on Paul Virilio's description of airports as gateways to the state.[5] Adey, in a manner that reflects entertainment media's preoccupation with airports and border security, argues that airports are not spaces of disinterest as mere infrastructure and operation. Airports act on bodies and minds;

they exert power and control by engaging and manipulating travelers and eliciting a range of emotions in the process of transit.[6] They are spaces imbued with state discourses promising efficiency in exchange for truth and authenticity, in which some travelers face more scrutiny than others.

Border-surveillance media narratives, as public histories of the airport, show that travelers from the Global South face greater consequences for security violations and more stringent conditions for entry than travelers from the Global North do. The decision about who gains entry and who does not is the primary affective and dramatic material of various interrelated border-security reality television shows. These shows exploit an association of migration and crime by linking mobility and processing at ports of entry with deception, smuggling, false identities, and fraud. Taken together, these media reflect the globalization of border policing and the integration of security networks across international organizations and agencies—intelligence, military, customs, and immigration control—to coordinate efforts and share data. This cooperation is enabled by technology and amplified by global surveillance cultures.

Global Borderveillant Media

The border-security reality television shows are not just popular; they are overwhelmingly successful in cultivating rapt and repeat audiences the world over. The original concept and most popular version of these shows hails from New Zealand, called simply *Border Patrol*. The show, created by the independent media company Greenstone in 2004, ran for eleven seasons and, in 2006, garnered the award for best reality television series at the New Zealand Screen Awards. When asked to comment on the show's popularity, producer Jani Alexander explained its appeal concisely in a manner related to the drama of law and order and border control: "I think people like to see that the border is protected."[7] *Border Patrol* documents the work of New Zealand Customs and Immigration and Ministry for Primary Industries agents at airports, mail facilities, and other places of transport. The show's format of interrelated stories, guided by border agents across varied spaces of security, set the template for other shows of its kind.

Border Patrol was so popular that it was replicated and franchised across other markets of the Five Eyes, particularly the equally popular and long-running show *Border Security: Australia's Front Line*, which began the same year in 2004; *Border Security: Canada's Front Line* (2012–2014); and *Border Security: America's Front Line* (2016–). All follow a format created by the Seven Network Australia. The Canadian version is produced by Vancouver-based Force Four Entertainment and appeared on the National Geographic channel. Across the world, a similar program, *UK Border Force*, predating the North American shows by several years, aired in 2008 and shares a distinction with the Canadian show. Both *UK Border Force* and *Border Security: Canada's Front Line* came under public scrutiny for violations in their operations. *UK Border Force* was met with controversy over the funding it received from the government through its Central Office of Information, while the Canadian show faced dire consequences for its privacy infractions.[8]

Border Security: Canada's Front Line is a beacon of popular resistance to the border-security regime as entertainment. It was canceled after public outrage ensued when federal officials, including the public safety minister, Vic Toews, allowed an immigration raid by the Canadian Border Services Agency (CBSA) to be filmed. The British Columbia Civil Liberties Association (BCCLA) filed a complaint against the CBSA on behalf of one of the targets of the raid, Oscar Mata Durán, who claimed that his privacy rights were violated. He was asked to sign a consent form under duress without fully understanding its terms or how the footage was going to be used; thus, his consent should not be considered valid. The government defended its position regarding the filming of the raid, inciting more public indignation. The activist Harsha Walia, known for her work against border imperialism, made a public statement against this action: "It is abhorrent that the federal government has adopted a private company to turn deportation into entertainment." She continued, presciently, "This U.S.-style raid and U.S.-style reality show only serves to promote fear."[9]

The public resistance to the show and its privacy violations led to a campaign in the form of a petition to cancel the program, addressed to, among others, the public safety minister and Force Four's presidents. The petition garnered tens of thousands of signatories from across Canada, including actors, directors, artists, advocacy groups, and Amnesty

International, which affirmed that "in *Border Security*, a highly one-sided narrative is told about those crossing the border under varying circumstances or those people in the process of migration, which has the particular long-term impact of spreading fear."[10] The Canadian Bar Association joined in the protest and urged the CBSA to rescind its agreement with the production company behind the show, Force Four, and asked that the show no longer film foreign nationals: "CBSA's participation in 'reality television' of this nature does not properly account for the impact of filming on a highly vulnerable population."[11] Walia's referencing of the US-style raid and reality TV form of the Canadian show acknowledges the lax privacy laws and "law and order" aesthetics of entertainment culture in the United States. While the protests in Canada succeeded in canceling the show, they did not change the global culture of border security and its exploitative dramas of enforcement. Like a hydra of villainy, the show reemerged in collaboration with US production companies on US soil with cooperation from the CBSA. The US version of the show features the US-Canadian border and is produced with the participation of the Province of British Columbia Film Incentive and the Canadian Film or Video Production Tax Credit by the Toronto-based global media company Entertainment One, which absorbed Force Four in 2014. The intimate partnership of the United States and Canada, by virtue of a shared border and a number of bilateral agreements and initiatives, is apparent in each version of the North American *Border Security* shows, evinced in scenarios of cooperation between the two border agencies. The cancellation of the Canadian show reveals the diverse status of privacy rights across the Five Eyes. However, consistent across all shows is the editorial rights granted to all respective border agencies in exchange for access to their operations for the purpose of filming commercial television.

The Australian version of *Border Security* is a direct outgrowth of its New Zealand forebear. A New Zealand production company, along with two Australian networks, proposed the show to Australian customs control, on the basis of the success of the original version. As mentioned in chapter 1, in the 2000s, the US entertainment market was replete with border-security programming focused on the US-Mexico border, particularly *Bordertown: Laredo* (A&E, 2011), *Border Wars* (National Geographic, 2010–2013), and *Law on the Border* (Animal Planet, 2012).

While *Border Wars* covers all aspects of US borders in its later seasons, it initially was entirely about the US-Mexico border. In 2016, with *Border Security: America's Front Line* (National Geographic), after a brief stint in 2009 with *Homeland Security: USA* (ABC, 2009), the United States reentered the global border-security market, focused on the production of security norms at ports of entry for multinational transit, notably airports and mail facilities.

The coordination of border security reflected in these shows emanates from a history of an expansive political matrix. This collaborative work is part of an ongoing alliance among the nations of the Five Eyes, an outcome of the 1943 pact of cooperation between the United States and the United Kingdom called the British-US agreement for intelligence gathering and sharing, BRUSA, which expanded to include "Anglo-Saxon members of the British Commonwealth."[12] The Five Eyes accord was formally accepted under the new name UKUSA in 1948. This international relationship, forged during World War II, continued beyond the war and is known as the "secret treaty" or tacit agreement that divides the world into corresponding areas of responsibility for each member state; however, the founding members maintain ultimate control over the network, with the US government maintaining its primacy.[13]

The intelligence gathering and sharing was formalized in the SIGINT agreement, or World War II–era signals intelligence, which evolved into the ECHELON program, the satellite-interception and data-gathering dragnet of civilian targets across a number of regions. Jeffrey Richelson notes the original area division of SIGINT: "The original division of responsibilities predated not only the creation of the Internet but the advent of satellite communications and space SIGINT collection. The United States was responsible for SIGINT in Latin America, most of Asia, Russia, and northern China. Australia's area of responsibility included its neighbors (such as Indonesia), southern China, and the nations of Indochina. Britain's responsibility included Africa and Russia west of the Urals. The polar regions of Russia were the responsibility of Canada, and New Zealand's area of responsibility was the western Pacific."[14] While each member nation shares in intelligence networks beyond this cooperative agreement, there is a clear cultural alliance and subsequent projection and establishment of security norms evident across the popular and political discourses of each of these five nations.

Indeed, the Five Eyes shared an "affinity strengthened by their common Anglo-Saxon culture, accepted liberal-democratic values and complementary national interests," which inspired among them a "profound sense of confidence in each other and a degree of professional trust so strong as to be unique in the world."[15] Moreover, the Five Eyes' areas of responsibility loosely correspond with the habits of transit and travel from the periphery or the Global South to the center, represented by each of these Anglo nations in the Global North. This correspondence is borne out in the narratives of a number of popular border-security television shows that show a preponderance of visitors and visa petitioners who correspond to each respective nation's "area of responsibility." In 2009, at "The Five Country Conference," the members of the Five Eyes reached an agreement to create a global network of shared visa-application centers and create a model for transnational immigration-policing practices. Though the agreement would not reshape patterns of migration, it transferred responsibility for authenticating the identities of petitioners to all member states. Through a data-sharing protocol, these visa centers process biometric data from multiple agencies to sort and identify travelers.[16] This coordination of data technologies is reflected in the global surveillance imaginary generated by the border-security programs across the alliance.

The *Border Security* franchise and its offshoots are a tacit outcome of the Five Eyes alliance as an outgrowth of the popular New Zealand forebear. All of these shows are about the various procedures for transiting through air, sea, and land ports, and all of them work to generate a similar affective atmosphere to make security operations reassuring, engaging, and even alluring for Global North audiences. They share in presenting the various theaters of entry and security processing, with particular attention to each nation's international airports. These shows are but one node in an expanding global capitalist infrastructure based on border security and emanating from the Five Eyes. They are also a product of the coordination and mutual observation and exchange between and among these global media markets. Elke Weissman notes that the exchange between the US and UK television markets is part of a wider geopolitical and geolinguistic market that includes, as noted earlier, Canada, Australia, and New Zealand, though the United States remains a market leader in exporting content.[17] Media scholars explore these relations according to various tributaries of the meaning of flow, particularly through the crosscurrents of content traffic among places, often along asymmetrical lines in a manner aligned with forms of power or influence based in market share. However, markets, as Timothy Havens has argued, do not tell the whole story.[18] The cultural affinities, and in this case the political alliances attendant to colonial histories, constitute a cornerstone of the Five Eyes media crosscurrent. The format of the security shows is replicated across the five nations, but aspects of the cultural context and subsequent content are distinct—for example, issues of biosecurity are more pronounced in some places than in others, and the national origins of unauthorized entry often reflect unique colonial or imperial dynamics. Moreover, this slate of borderveillant programming runs counter to the standard US centrifugal flow, with a less powerful market, New Zealand, leading the charge, taking up the security protocol of the leading powers of the United States and the United Kingdom. Regardless of difference, all the shows promote a particular version of border security at the intersection of entertainment and governmentality, premised on the affective dynamics between border agents and travelers and shaped by the logic of the surveillant sort.

Mark Andrejevic locates borderveillant shows at the intersection of the media and the state, with reference to *Border Security: Australia's Front Line*, and describes them as "securitainment," a post-9/11 invention in which the public is recruited into state security initiatives. The interface of security and entertainment enacts the logic of neoliberalism, while it evinces the alliance of the government with the private sector.[19] In fact, as mentioned in chapter 1, Peter Hughes analyzes *Border Security: Australia's Front Line* as a function of the neoliberal state. These programs are a result of their actual alliance with government agencies while mobilizing support for their work as a form of public relations, or what Catherine Deveney calls their "documentary/advertisement/propaganda" function.[20] Hughes views the program as a means of controlling the risks that arise as a consequence of increased mobility in a globalized world. Risk is managed through public exposure to the security process, particularly in "normalizing regimes of knowledge, technical procedures and modes of judgement and sanction related to national security and boundary maintenance."[21] Border agents normalize the security regime through their interactions with the public in the show and beyond it. The normalizing process unfolds in the interpersonal dynamic of agents and travelers in the customs interview.

These shows share a common approach to border security, premised on human affect and the individual work of each agent to extract the true identity of persons and their belongings through appeals to moral rectitude or threat of consequence, illustrating the coercive force of surveillance and its social context of enactment. Travelers negotiate with agents, some attempt to manipulate or deceive officers, and all are ultimately unsuccessful—those who are successful do not appear on these shows. Many of these stories are about the flexible boundary between truth-telling and deceit and the efforts to clarify the difference. On *Border Patrol*, for example, a man attempting to visit New Zealand from the United States is detained for neglecting to admit to a criminal record on his declaration form. He argues that the criminal record contradicts his own self-assessment that he is good and law-abiding and that the past does not determine future actions. He argues that he made "mistakes" that were the result of the reckless and immature behavior of a nineteen-year-old. Yet he is denied entry for deception and false statements, regardless of having served his time. He is marked as criminal, and his failure to acknowledge this further defines his criminality, making him unfit for entry to New Zealand.

While this traveler was denied entry for false reporting, a great majority of the travelers to New Zealand, Australia, and the United Kingdom are denied entry or fined for failing to declare items that pose a threat to the ecological balance of each island nation. In the case of New Zealand's *Border Patrol*, the intersection of border-patrol practices with ecological concerns rehearses aspects of similar discourses along the "wild" US-Mexico border. In the Southwest, migrants are inculpated for disruption of a vulnerable desert ecosystem, the blame for which is displaced from border-security infrastructure and vehicles—including helicopters and all-terrain vehicles—onto migrants' passage, whose foot traffic and detritus are erroneously deemed a greater source of environmental degradation. The border-security imaginary of *Border Patrol* conveys the fragility of the New Zealand ecosystem through the language of biosecurity surveillance. Sarina Pearson describes how the show indulges a fantasy of a serene and untouched paradise ambushed and abused by criminally careless itinerants. This image is discursively produced; we do not see many aspects of the outside landscape of the island nation. The action remains in the airport terminal, inside mail facilities, and at marine ports. Pearson writes, "Without so much as an image of a tree, mountain, stream, or beach, audiences are in no doubt that the landscape under ubiquitous and constant threat is pristine and natural."[22] All items subject to review are processed with attention to their destructive potential and invasive capacities. Often, across all of these shows of the Five Eyes, travelers carry foods and spices from their national cuisines that fail to meet agricultural or public-health standards in the Global North. Their food items are regarded as curiosities and pungent signs of the less cultivated and sophisticated tastes and practices of travelers from the Global South.

The biosecurity principles of border security, in mediated worlds, align cultural tastes with juridical norms around immigration. Agents describe confiscating food items that might contain "undocumented stowaways." On the US version of the *Border Security* series, agriculture specialists in secondary inspection describe their search for a "tiny eco-terrorist," the Capra beetle from the Middle East, which poses a threat as a "destructive, invasive species." In the same series, agents' disgust at travelers' attempt to ferry uncooked pigeon carcass across the border, described as a violation of ecological law and public health, is more forcefully expressed as a violation of US cultural norms of good taste. These instances are taken as proof that biosecurity, border security, and surveillance are not practiced consistently in the Global South and that the North should continue to shape global norms of discernment between invasive and native species, good and bad migrants, and legal and illegal forms of entry. In much the same way that migrants are framed as agents of contamination and invasive species along the US-Mexico border, travelers from the Global South entering the countries of the Global North are under scrutiny for their potential contagion to the national body.

Object Lessons: Tale of Two Bananas

In *Border Security: America's Front Line*, biosecurity concerns are less urgent, and unlike the case with the New Zealand–based program, they operate without the backdrop of an idyllic and vulnerable landscape.

The US version focuses on airport travel to and from John F. Kennedy Airport in New York City and Chicago's O'Hare International Airport and associates the continent with urbanity rather than environmental vulnerability—the security imaginary would be closer to that of New Zealand if the show were to take place at the Daniel K. Inouye International Airport in Honolulu, but large metropoles on the continent are deemed more iconic, thus metonymic, of the nation. Nonetheless, travelers originating from international destinations are prohibited from carrying organic materials into the United States. These rules are applied consistently, but the ramifications for their violations are doled out arbitrarily, that is, according to an unwritten or tacit logic related to a surveillance regime of truth and travelers' rapport with individual agents.

Across all of these shows, and implicit to the surveillance cultures at ports of entry, visitors must be absolutely, as Rachel Hall notes, transparent.[23] They must expose their belongings to inspection and exhibit the proper comportment and affective response. If traveling with contraband, they must confess, and if caught, they must show appropriate and authentic remorse. Resistance in the form of deception, lack of repentance, manipulation, or skeptical questioning of policies is suspect and typically results in greater consequences. On the US version of the show, there are two cases that are similar with regard to the violation of security protocol but that yield entirely different outcomes based on the affective response and demeanor of the traveler. These two cases from the first season of the show are not presented in the same episode, so any continuity between them is accidental. In the first instance, at Chicago's O'Hare International Airport, a CBP officer questions a Ukrainian national residing in the United States and returning from abroad. The agent describes the traveler as evasive and avoiding eye contact; he is taciturn and even resistant. The traveler claims he has nothing save some caramels to declare, though the first items the officer encounters upon opening his bag are two bananas. The traveler is admonished for not declaring the bananas, and his response is skeptical disbelief: "Declare bananas, why?" He follows with "two bananas, no big deal," to which the officer objects. The traveler challenges the officer, asking if it is necessary to open his bags without cause. He is informed that CBP officers have full legal sanction to search his belongings at will. During the process of the search, he is mollified, and his curmudgeonly attitude turns playful and cooperative. His bananas are confiscated, and he is allowed entry and even jokes with the cameraman that he is fine even though his stuff was "stolen."

In the second case of the contraband bananas, a US American woman returning from Thailand neglects to declare bananas that she claims she forgot were packed in her bag. The officer informs her that she has to know the contents of her bag when she travels, "especially in this day and age with a lot of bad people trying to do bad things to the United States." The traveler responds that she does not share this worldview and is "not into that fear mode." Her defiance makes her subject to a penalty for failure to declare: she is fined, and her bags are subject to closer inspection. She is outraged in her exit interview: "I forget I have bananas in my bag, and I go through this interrogation process as if I'm a criminal carrying drugs. A lousy banana." The agent informs us of the gravity of the case, of the potential for the banana to carry insects or disease, requiring her to enforce the law to prevent such catastrophes.

These two scenarios of undeclared bananas are similar but yield diverse outcomes. Perhaps the targeting of the two travelers ferrying contraband bananas accords with the status of the countries from which their travels originate: areas of the Global South are deemed as requiring more processing and review. Yet these two cases of contraband bananas reveal the power of petty sovereigns to adjudicate cases according to their subjective interpretation of the law in a manner that appears arbitrary, though agents make decisions on behalf of the state on the basis of laws and techniques of governmentality that they neither author nor fully control. Airport security encounters involve a complex calculation of risk factors, assessed in a manner that is not automatic but may appear to be so. Agents must make sovereign decisions in a manner that reveals what Brian Massumi calls the "lightning strike" of power and that Louise Amoore further distinguishes as the "sovereign strike" of borderline decisions about entry, asylum, and deportation. These are decisions deemed empty or automatic, but for Amoore, they are "teeming with life, technique, art, technology, violence, resistance, potentiality."[24] Indeed, this affective, political, and technical mix of forces energizes border-security narratives.

The only difference between the two cases of errant bananas is the decision-making agent and the disposition of the traveler. Each traveler carries a banana and does not declare it, though the man returning from Ukraine knows he has bananas in his bag, did not declare them, and refuses to acknowledge the gravity of this transgression. The woman returning from Thailand had no memory of the banana in her possession. Yet the woman questions the entire security apparatus, its basis in fear and anticipated risk, and the fundamental suspiciousness attributed to all travelers. She is punished with fines and confiscation for failure to be sufficiently docile.

Across all of these border-security shows of the Five Eyes, viewers are acculturated to the affective landscape of the surveillance regime; the particularities of each national-security code are less important than proper disposition that, while aligned with the truth regime, requires docility to the security state. Even if travelers are initially resistant, as with the man returning from Ukraine, they must eventually conform to the regime, submit to its protocol, and accept its procedures. These shows train audiences in proper comportment at international borders. Truthfulness, while tantamount, is joined by docility as a cardinal value of migrants transiting the global security regime. Travelers learn more than just how to abide the techniques of security; there is an entire lesson about the global order inherent to airport transit. Mika Aaltola describes the movement through international airports as part of the "pedagogy of American empire," in which transit inculcates political fundamentals about the hierarchical global system. The airport, once a monument to global modernity, is an emblem of a post-9/11 imperial order in which the world's airports are nodes in US empire's expanded borders. These international hubs are sites of differentiation where Global North travelers are pedagogical and moral guides.[25] The drama of the airport, readily displayed across the mediated worlds of border-security shows, inculcates the moral distinction and separation between the traveler from the Global North and the migrant, refugee, underdocumented, or overdocumented traveler from the Global South.

Gateway to the State

The airport is entirely different from the territorial border, particularly that between the United States and Mexico, a borderlands space layered with histories of movement, struggle, settlement, and shifting ecologies. Airports lack such historical depth; they are what Marc Auge describes as "non-places," like other inventions of "super-modernity" that are not born of other spaces but, as mere space, are transit points and temporary way stations marked by the temporality of the ephemeral. Auge's non-places of supermodernity are not utopias, sites that are mostly imagined and unreal.[26] Instead, they are closer to Certeau's notion of space as a site of mobility and transit transformed by those whose temporary occupations exert forces on it.[27] The non-place conjures the abstraction of readily transposable symbolic sites, in the way that airports in diverse locations around the world, like those in the docuseries of the Five Eyes, share characteristics and qualities that shape similar experiences of each space. Their symbolic significances are circumscribed by their capitalist orientations and design for commercial and contractual ends. Thus, for Auge, the non-place is the "opposite of utopia: it exists."[28] Borders of all kinds share the character of non-places, where the conditions of anonymity demand proof of identity. The non-place can only be entered by the "innocent," who surrenders to the role of passenger as part of the codes of transaction: "The passenger through non-places retrieves his [sic] identity only at Customs, at the toll booth, at the check-out counter. . . . The space of non-place creates neither singular identity nor relations; only solitude, and similitude."[29] There is no history, community, sociality, or solidarity at the airport; it is defined entirely by the exigencies of security and exists in the present moment—though it was a vital site of resistance during the Muslim ban in the United States. While theorists of the airport, particularly Peter Adey, take issue with the description of the airport as a non-place, arguing that it is a space shaped by affect and experience, aspects of the description of the airport in its abstraction are useful for considering how it replicates particular kinds of experiences across the Five Eyes and for its contrast to the historically embedded space of the US-Mexico borderlands.[30]

In Alastair Gordon's cultural history of the airport, he notes the emergence of airport design commonplaces that arise as much from technological standards for symmetry of runway alignment and hangar communication as from the psychosocial demands for passenger spaces designed to alleviate the anxiety and tensions of travel. Airports are monuments of the machine age that signal entry into modernity through the adventure of air travel. Most airports in the United States followed a late-1920s configuration, modeled on the Ford Airport in Dearborn, Michigan, designed by Albert Kahn, that favored symmetry along with a separate depot for travelers that would shelter them from noxious fumes and noise from the aviation works.[31] Airport design evolved to include technologies of control to shape travelers' passage through a built environment with equal attention to safety, security, control, and consumerism. Airports are sites for imagining and disseminating the globalization of a security regime. The shared design imaginary and philosophy of airports contributes to the placelessness or transposability of the experience of this space. In the shows about port security across the Five Eyes, the experience of the airport is readily translatable to other global locations.

Each show foregrounds the airport encounter as the nodal human drama of the series. The complexity of the security apparatus at the airport is crystallized in a single dynamic and social relation of agent to traveler, of state to migrant. The airport border joins the territorial border as symbolic of state control of mobility and the distinctions of social sorting. The cornerstone series of the genre, *Border Patrol*, begins by framing the drama at the Auckland International Airport with an imposing image of major-airline jets, emphasizing both the monumentality of the airport and the power of the machine, and the border agents on the ground who act as "gatekeepers" protecting "New Zealand's way of life." This is a common image and framing of international airports in the various series of the Five Eyes. Each associates the airport with an industrial futurism of speed, mobility, and total security. The Auckland airport is a postmodern complex in which the exoskeleton of the main building is composed of its machinic infrastructure, similar in style to the O'Hare International Airport, Toronto Pearson International Airport, Sydney International Airport, and the Heathrow International Airport. Each is a monument to global travel, and in each show, the exterior of the airport, along with shots of international jets, introduces scenes of processing and surveillance of global travelers by state agents. A common technique of fast-paced editing of sped-up, time-lapsed scenes of passengers moving through terminals lends a visceral sense of the magnitude and volume of travel through each airport. Accompanying these scenes are short takes of control rooms full of screens of footage from cameras from all over the airport, reminding viewers of the total surveillance of these enclosures. In all of these airports and shows, free-ranging border agents monitor crowds, looking for anyone who appears nervous or exhibits any affect out of the norm of calm composure—as in the case of one traveler, a woman of color, in *Border Patrol* who is taken aside for the appearance of having "an attitude." She is taken to a "red zone," or what the US and Canadian shows refer to as "secondary," a separate, often depopulated wait area or office to which the traveler is taken for further processing and questioning.

These processing zones are bare spaces with scant national markings, save some touristic images or Native art—as in the case of the Auckland International Airport—of the nation that each airport serves. All of these spaces share the same mood as sites of surveillance that, even as audiences are granted access through these shows, are off-limits to public view. Access to the security footage, as off-scene, private, unseen images to which we are typically not privy, is part of what makes these shows alluring. Air travel, while often banal and accessible to many more people than when commercial air transit was first introduced, is also a highly secured activity. While these shows remind us of the security environment of air travel, they also present a ubiquity of cameras capturing every element of this security experience.

Border Patrol reveals the clear boundary separating legal from unlawful image capture at the airport. In a dramatic scene, a man traveling from Brazil to New Zealand is caught surreptitiously filming at the airport with a spy-like camera pen. The show unironically covertly films him filming covertly. In what is played for high spy drama, he is taken to the "red zone" to review footage that is much like the footage of the show itself but from the point of view of the traveler facing the airport surveillance regime. The agents analyze the video and after some deliberation ultimately deem it benign within the context of his desire to self-surveil, to document every aspect of his travel for social media. His surveillance of the airport is banal, not intended for some other pernicious plan. He is allowed entry into the country, and his case is yet another lesson in security protocol and the importance of agents' discernment for travelers' admission.

Viewers of the border-surveillance shows are trained to discern who should be allowed entry and who should not. The preface to *UK Border*

Force suggests that the action of the show occurs with visitors who are part of the latter group, those who are not "welcome and legal": "Every year over one hundred million people go through passport control to get into Britain. Most are welcome and legal. Many are not. For the first time on television, we go behind the scenes of the UK Border Agency, the men and women on the front line of immigration." A preponderance of travelers to the United Kingdom featured on the show are "clandestines," or undocumented migrants from the Global South, including the Indian subcontinent, Afghanistan, Iraq, Africa, and non-EU countries in eastern Europe. Most of the show is devoted to targeting migrants from the Global South, discovering their deception or unlawful presence, and then arresting, detaining, and deporting them. Border processing mingles indistinctly with policing. This is apparent when the border agent Lisa Leigh, who has "developed an eye for things that don't add up," uses her "power" to search luggage or when agents of the enforcement team exert their power to enter private homes and arrest migrants, initiating the proceedings toward deportation.

UK Border Force, a Sky TV series, is the outcome of the collaboration between the UK Border Force and the independent production company Steadfast Television. It was initially sponsored by the Home Office, but after public outrage, those funds were returned to ensure the public of the independence of the show. It appeared in 2008 and reflects the plan of then minister of state for borders and immigration Phil Woolas to create the "biggest shake up" of border security in the United Kingdom.[32] The series broadcasts and dramatizes the messages of the state on issues of immigration and border enforcement, particularly in the expansion of migration control beyond ports of entry. The British show departs from others of its kind for its many forays beyond the airport and into the communities where undocumented migrants work and live to arrest and detain them—though it should be noted that *Border Security: Canada's Front Line* episodically features Inland Enforcement agents, who work beyond the border regions often in collaboration with local and federal police and US agencies. *UK Border Force* shows how undocumented migrants work and live in communities and how readily the state might extract and deport them. It aligns more closely with US shows about the southern border, such as *Border Wars* and *Law on the*

Border, in which agents infiltrate communities to enforce immigration policies, revealing the expansion of the border regime into daily life.

UK Border Force is unique in another way. It reveals how the British immigration regime exports the border all over the world, to 135 countries, where British immigration staff vet those who seek to travel to the island. The audience has visual access to the global immigration network beyond the customs interview, for instance, to the port at Calais, a common transit point to the United Kingdom, or to busy immigration offices in India. The imperial border is one that is ubiquitous and omnipotent; it is mobile and malleable and has the power to seek out, sort, and extract migrants no matter the location.

Border Intimacies

The drama of these shows is entirely premised on the tension created in the process of adjudicating travelers' worthiness of entry through the power to revoke visas and deport any petitioner at will. Ports of entry in border spaces are sites of control that exert the power of restriction on mobility in exchange for truth, docility, and authenticity. The decisions, as depicted in these stories, have yet to be automated and are of a historical moment that depends on the melodrama of the intimate interpersonal dynamic between traveler and border agent. While the technology for nonhuman mediation exists, it would make for a decidedly less dramatic entertainment. These stories, typically several interwoven narratives that conclude with agents' adjudication about entry, compel the audience's interest for their narrative intrigue and suspense. According to the executive producer of *Border Security: Australia's Front Line*, Lyndal Marks, the show's appeal emanates from its unfolding mystery in watching the "anatomy of a lie," as the traveler under suspicion is investigated. Likewise, the theme music for *Border Security: Canada's Front Line*, "Would I Lie to You?" by the Eurythmics, is the anthem of a deceitful lover and establishes the primacy of detecting deception and fraud within the intimate dynamics of border-patrol work. Marks notes that the entertainment value of the show, and of all of these series, is a consequence of the range of emotions elicited in this process of unraveling the truth.[33]

We are drawn into the narrative world of the airport interview for the unfolding plot and suspense toward final resolution. Most often we await outcomes related to travelers who have little or no luggage or excessive luggage, who have too much or too little legal documentation, who are visiting serious romantic partners in the United States on tourist visas (rather than K1 "fiancé" visas), who have dubiously sourced items in their possession, who plan on staying for more than a few weeks without a work visa, or who make many short trips to the same place that holds no overt family, intimate, or professional connection. Many travelers are targeted for review for their transit from known drug-source countries and some for their suspicious appearance, a preponderance of whom are from countries in the Global South and appear "foreign" or non-White.

Borders and border surveillance evoke the technologies of processing identities at ports of entry in a manner that draws on networks of information shared between and among states. Bodies themselves are transformed into information, or data doubles.[34] On these shows, our attention is not on data transfer but on the action, expressed in the interpersonal and professional dynamic between the travelers and the agents. We are not allowed access to the information networks or databases, nor do we have any idea about the various routes and flows of information. We only see the work of the petty sovereign and the reaction of the detained traveler. The agent's role and main goal in each interaction across these stories is limited to determining the veracity of the traveler's declaration and, in some cases, of their documents and purported identity. The entire surveillance apparatus is a truth regime in which truth value is adjudicated by the agents, whose subjective application of the rules is shaped by their personal disposition and the sociocultural context in which they are located.

The show *Borderline* (Channel 5, 2016–), a subversive mockumentary from the United Kingdom, is a consequence of the popularity of border-security reality TV shows and a significant insurrection against the regime of truth at the airport. While it is not part of the slate of border-surveillance media proper, it is a telling symptom of the genre that exposes the major preoccupations and standard tropes of the docuseries. *Borderline* takes place at a fictional small, regional airport in the United Kingdom populated with many of the stock characters of the airport security shows. Unlike these shows, it broaches the topic of the securitization of gender identity as it intersects with the search for "truth." In particular, it shows how gender identity is documented in the passport through key points of data that subject the body to invasive surveillance.[35] In the episode "Transgender," a passenger is held for questioning about the mismatch between their gender presentation and the gender marker on their passport (season 2, episode 4). The comedy ensues from the cisgender-male border agent's complete ineptness and discomfort at encountering a transgender passenger, Alicia Barnes, played by trans activist Nicole Gibson. Barnes left the United Kingdom on a passport designating one gender and now returns with another gender identity. The border agent asks the passenger if she is "attempting to travel on somebody else's passport" and becomes bewildered when the response is negative. He takes her into secondary, where the agent tries to verify what he calls "the whole Alec/Alicia interface thing." He then tries to convince the traveler to identify with the gender designation on the passport simply to facilitate entry. Justifiably enraged, Alicia demands a lawyer.

Borderline challenges the security regime's demand for gender binarism and gender stability, while it shows how questions about legal documentation play out for those whose gender identity does not match that on their government-issued documents. It exposes Barnes's justified outrage at being detained, questioned, scrutinized, and criminalized. This episode reveals the crisis in state regulation of gender, what Lisa Jean Moore and Paisley Currah note as the abiding "cultural concern about the truth and permanence of sex and gender."[36] As a fictional narrative, *Borderline* subverts the rigidity of security protocol and the absurdity in demanding compliance and bodily complicity with legal documents. Any deviation to documented gender identity is considered a transgression and subjects travelers to detention and further scrutiny.

At the airports featured in these programs, once travelers are caught in a transgression, they might admit to wrongdoing or insist on their innocence or ignorance of the rules, and agents have the power to decide to detain them, send them back, or allow them entry. The shows' appeal is not only, as the producer of *Border Patrol* opines, in seeing the border protected but also in the social, cultural, and personal dynamics of the interview. The interview is a drama infused with the workings of power, manipulation, fear, and submission. The traveler is a desiring

Figure 4.1. Transparency and truth at the airport in
Border Security: Australia's Front Line. (Netflix,
2014–2015)

subject, seeking entry, while the agent has the power of refusal. The
human dimension of border surveillance through assessment and discernment of the truth is facilitated by technology but never replaced by
it. The agent's role cannot be automated; such a turn of events would
obviate much of the interest in these shows.

Truth and truth-telling are the key tropes of these programs. Emma
Price and Amy Nethery describe how the sociocultural attitudes and
norms around truth-telling guide the way agents adjudicate cases on
Border Security: Australia's Front Line. Discourses of veracity and authenticity shape the show's storytelling according to national politics.
Audiences gauge the truthfulness of travelers in much the same way
that they gauge the authenticity of the show. They seek nothing less
than transparency and verisimilitude. While truthfulness is a key con-

dition across border-security shows, the Australian example points to a key difference in the cultural meaning of the term in relation to immigration policies. Price and Nethery describe the primacy of truth as an Australian cultural value and part of the national myth: "Australians understand themselves as a 'genuine' people: they are 'fair dinkum,' 'for real,' 'direct,' and have an attuned 'bullshit detector.' Australians are generous and compassionate, but not so much that it allows them to be 'taken for a ride.' If newcomers are 'straight' or truthful with authorities about the circumstances of their entry into Australia, and their entry is legal, then they will be welcomed. Anything less than truthful means that newcomers have failed one of the key rules of behavior and a test for inclusion in the Australian community."[37] The national character as understood by common myths in everyday discourse is contradictory, at once truth-telling and direct and, as the authors note, not in a manner that is maverick but one that is rule-abiding. Truthfulness contains its own obfuscations and marginalizing processes. Across the Five Eyes, it is linked to language facility in English and clarity of self-expression, for which those who exhibit English as a second dialect or as a second language maintain a distinct disadvantage. Those who are not proficient in English might be deemed inscrutable subjects whose lapses in grammar and diction might be associated with deceit. They are often unable to convincingly disabuse agents of their purported deceptions, particularly if their language is not represented on the customs declaration cards.

Truth-telling in the Australian example is clearly tied to a body politic defined by typologies of inclusion and exclusion around immigration. This is linked to totemic moments in Australian immigration histories in which migrants seeking refugee status were accused of deception, concealing true impetuses of economic exile. The border-surveillance regime has shifted the evidentiary criteria for refugee status to that of ferreting out deception and other darker motives related to terrorism. The result of this process is a reversion to nativism, what Roderic Pitty and Michael Leach describe as Australia's "regressive nationalism," the enabling condition for shows about controlling national borders.[38]

The demand for truth and for adherence to the law subtends an authoritarian ideology of law and order. Audiences seek stories about creative forms and means of deception but only if there are equally creative ways of detecting falsehoods. These same audiences take pleasure in witnessing the human assertion of rules and the execution of justice, defined as "letting the right ones in." The characters on these shows, actual people working and traveling, fit into a melodramatic moral universe of good versus bad, of good agents in search of bad migrants.

These shows provide tutelage in border imperialism and training protocol and cautionary guides for proper comportment at international ports of entry. In fact, the Canadian version of the show, though canceled for legal reasons, was so popular that the network continues to explore resurrecting it. In the network's assessment of the impact and allure of the series through surveying audiences, it found that much of public knowledge of security protocol at ports of entry can be traced to the show.

The border-security docuseries are powerful training tools. They demonstrate how to be docile and self-regulating objects of border security; as such, they are symptoms of the security apparatus, its policies and technologies, in practice. These shows produce a culture of security through the mimetic power of the optical regime that acculturates viewers to security and screening protocol. Their proximity to reality lends them the character of history, making them appear part of the historical record of the immigration process of each nation, one that is ideologically skewed to the right and edited to create compelling story lines about catching potential criminals in the act of deception, fraud, or illegal trespass. These shows present their borders as protected zones that are continually defended; taken together, the borders are defended in concert as historical artifacts of the Five Eyes agreement. The drama of the imperial border is a story of past trespass, of attempted security breaches that accrue to repeating trends that we see over and over, enabling and reflecting the seriality of each show. These repeat stories are functions of the past. The story of the future border unfolds in other realms and genres, in strategic plans, projections, predictions, and speculative dreams.

5

Border Futures

Seeing and Foreseeing

Borders have been long deemed the blueprints for our surveillance futures—or surveillance societies. Sites of highly
contentious and visible forms of screening and scrutiny, borders are now the exemplar of futuristic and high-tech security fantasies.
—Peter Adey, "Borders, Identification and Surveillance"

The border dividing the U.S. from Mexico is subject to a
wide variety of future possibilities. Increasing the unique nature of its circumstances are the varying studies that assert
the region's potential for prosperity, development, and environmental entrepreneurship—proof that the U.S.-Mexico
border could serve as a global model for positive change in
the future.
—Fernando Romero/LAR, *Hyperborder*

This place is the future.
—William, *Westworld*

The US Customs and Border Protection and its global counterparts
maintain a hegemonic view of the border future, shaped by the grammar
of desire and expressed in the wish to complete the unfinished project of
total surveillance and control of movement through all ports of entry.
Or as mentioned in an earlier chapter, the border future is one described
by the Republican senator Kay Bailey Hutchison, in which "round-the-
clock surveillance [is] the standard for all 2,000 miles of the U.S.-Mexico
border."[1] This projection indexes a single vision of the border as a for-
tress and absolute limit. There might be innumerable possible border

futures, from a world without borders to a borderlands without barriers, from binational bridges to interconnected enclaves to parks and shared built environments for purposes other than security and exclusion. The US southern border and borders in general are screens for projecting speculative futures from various ideological vantages. The border future is historically embedded and links diverse media and discourses, from science fiction, design, and modeling to the future-oriented work of policy and planning.

Borders evoke the temporal and spatial collapse of the meaning of "frontiers" as sites beyond the horizon of the present. Peter Adey describes borders as intimately related to the future and ripe with surveillance fantasies, a perfect screen for the fantasy of social control.[2] The US homeland-security imaginary in its strategic-plan futurism designates borders, including the iconic territorial US-Mexico border, as the final technological frontier for state power. The border evokes competing imagined futures; one version, from the point of view of the state, emphasizes prediction and preemption for complete control, while on the other hand, border regimes have no future: they are abolished in favor of an emancipatory vision of freedom of movement. The will to enact a borderless future is a function of what Nick Montfort calls the imaginative work of "future-making," one that is not concerned with prediction and reaction but with creation, with creative works shaped by common goals of progress and liberation.[3] This future need not be entirely imaginary and may comprise plans for a "practical utopia" or a "real utopia." Erik Olin Wright describes the latter as "institutional designs that simultaneously attempt to embody emancipatory ideals in a serious way while still being attentive to the practical problems of viability and sustainability."[4] The future border imaginary is created in the process of "prefiguration," or the vision that guides the creation of a reconstructed social reality so that, according to Harsha Walia, "the methods we practice, the institutions we create and relationships we facilitate within our movements and communities reflect and align with activist ideals."[5] Walia notes, citing Robin D. G. Kelley, the importance of building toward a different future. For Kelley, we might find new paths out of oppressive conditions through the creative possibilities of dreaming. Yet he argues for some form of figuration, creative modeling, or envisioning to shape these dreams, since "without new visions we don't know what to build, only what to knock down. We not only end up confused, rudderless, and cynical, but we forget that making a revolution is not a series of clever maneuvers and tactics but a process that can and must transform us."[6] These are but a few strands of the variegated and diverse forms of future-oriented thinking, from futurology to critical future studies, from the future promised by technologies capable of reaching far beyond human capacities and the speculative fictions of utopic or dystopic visions to the planned futures of military-corporate alliances and the activist visions for social transformation. This chapter explores possible futures of and beyond the surveillant imaginary of the Global North through the various popular imaginings, artistic creations, visions, and speculative fictions about national frontiers and borders real and imagined.

Border-Security Futurism

In the United States, popular fascination with the future exploded in July 1970 with the "runaway bestseller" by Alvin Toffler, *Future Shock*. The book's jacket copy presents its case concisely: "*Future Shock* is about the present." It is about the dizzying technocultural changes, particularly the acceleration of time and compression of space, planned obsolescence, "information overload," overabundance of choice, and the upending of traditional values, or "value vertigo," to which readers were struggling to adjust. *Future Shock* is about shock to the familiar and known; it marks the dizzying experience of confronting the unknown and the unknowable. The future is presented as a vexing cultural ill for which *Future Shock* offers a diagnosis. The remedy is found in the science of futurism through prognosticating and planning to "create reliable images of the most probable future."[7] Futurism would evolve to become known in popular discourses as the mapping and forecasting of the science of prediction. Yet, for the futurologist Max Dublin, writing in the shadow of *Future Shock*, the science of prediction and preemption would become its own ailment.

Dublin's *Futurehype*, published in 1990, twenty years after Toffler's blockbuster tome, responds to the ongoing cultural obsession with futurology in North America. Toffler and Dublin are among popular mainstream writers of future studies; both provide cultural diagnoses of ailments related to the intensification of speculative projections while shaping a popular cultural understanding of the meaning of futures. Dublin critiques the cultural preoccupation with prophecy and prediction in a study unburdened by the language of predictive policing or the algorithmic fervor of contemporary surveillance culture. Dublin argues that "the relationship between prediction and military affairs has always been so strong that it is safe to say that if futurology did not now exist, the military, in its characteristically determined way, would probably be trying to invent it."[8] He depicts the mission and objectives of the military's strategic plans, along with its futurist preoccupations with prediction, forecasting of outcomes, and prevention of the dreaded "surprise attack" by a better armed and prepared enemy. After World War II, these calculations moved from the domain of the military to "scientists and accountants" charged with the dubious mission of "madly dashing towards the future in order to close fictitious gaps" in weaponry and nuclear capability. Dublin challenges the popular obsession with prediction in the realm of military affairs: "Military futurology both reflects our obsession with trying to perfect the calculability of the incalculable and epitomizes the destructive, destabilizing, and paralytic role that futurology generally plays in human affairs."[9]

Futurology generates ideological prophets who use illusory means, mystifications, and baseless prognostics to forecast aspects of the unknown. Predictive forms of surveillance are beset by presumptions about the incalculable future and charged by anxieties about social transformation. Likewise, the border future promulgated by the CBP is limited by a single vision and circumscribed by an anxious desire for total surveillance and automatic border control. The global border-security regime seeks to predict and control for risk and threat to maintain the status quo in a divided world order. Its future is limited by a failure of imagination and circumscribed by a restrictive and exclusionary logic based in neoliberal forms of racial capitalism. The future of complete border control is one of intensified social inequities in which mobility belongs to the wealthy and connected and supports and sustains the power of the Global North.

In the United States, border-security futurism is simultaneously advanced and historically grounded; it is imbued with the fantasies of Old Western frontiers and charged by the simple moral values of good cowboys, Texas Rangers, and Border Patrol versus bad bandits, migrants, and "narcoterrorists." This future is mapped in the *CBP Strategy 2020–2025: Mission/Team/Future.* Strategic plans are speculative, establishing a blueprint for future action. The CBP plan enumerates three main goals that coalesce around mission and team building, but it is the final goal, designated under the rubric "future," that evinces the clearest sense of border-security futurism. The latter contains three interrelated initiatives: data and analytics, IT infrastructure, and global partnerships toward building the CBP future: "To build our future, CBP will take concerted efforts to harness and apply the power of data, intelligence, and advanced analytics, develop and maintain top-quality IT infrastructure and access, and expand our international and intelligence partnerships to leverage the benefit of interoperability and collaboration. Through these investments, personnel will be able to make decisions based on timely information informed by quality data, intelligence, and analytics, and be able to access the technology they need to do their job."[10] The main objective of the plan is to create a "counter network" capable of "identifying, degrading and disrupting" criminal networks through predictive data analytics to "stop threats before they arrive at U.S. borders."[11] The images that accompany this future plan are of advanced technologies, from ground-level surveillance, represented by the Tethered Aerostat Radar System (TARS), to aerial surveillance, depicted through a small, unmanned aircraft (UAS), along with images of field operations, with agents on the ground "fast-roping," or landing from a helicopter—again suggesting the embeddedness of the history of Border Patrol agents as cowboy heroes in the technofuturism of the CBP.

In the border future, agents are technocowboys steeped in the mythos of the West who deploy drones, ground sensors, and radar along with analog forms of tracking their targets. While this might seem like an unimaginable ahistorical mélange, the television show *Westworld* (HBO, 2016–) nicely captures the archaic and anachronistic ethos of border-security futurism along with the forms of resistance that appear within it. *Westworld*'s future is projected onto the Old West and its borders, the boundaries of which align with the national border of the United States where it abuts Mexico to the south. The future border is a true dystopia; it is a place where inhabitants are subjugated to the violent desires of the Global North in a state of total corporate-state control and surveillance,

Figure 5.1. William asserts dominion in *Westworld*. ("The Original," *Westworld*, season 1, episode 1, 2016)

one that trades on docile and stateless labor. The border future of *Westworld* is a symptom of the sociopolitical context of the present; it is not a politically neutral imaginary.

Westworld is a theme park created by the Delos corporation. It is a speculative space for the fantasies of the settler colonialists, embodied by the corporate owners of a technofuturistic western-themed playground and its tourist visitors. Westworld is a southwestern town framed by rock formations that were iconized during the golden age of the western, populated by robot hosts, and run by a stable of programmers located "off-world" beyond the borders of the tourist bubble, which is shot in various southwestern locations, including Moab, Utah; Monument Valley, Arizona; and Gateway, Colorado. The town caters to the desires of its vacationing visitors, who seek the thrills of the lawless, unsettled era of the nation. Tourists, male and female, visit frontier towns and engage in all their mythic vices; they cavort with and abuse women, drink excessively, gamble, and shoot to kill their hosts without consequence. The hosts are mere "code" in human-shaped flesh whose labor is to enact the exploitative fantasies of the vacationers without consciousness of insult, abuse, or injury. The future of labor is robotic nonconsciousness, pure data in human form, controlled off-site by programmers who create a frictionless and unequal social order under permanent surveillance— this future labor is uncompensated, delegitimized, stateless, docile, and deeply vulnerable and finds its analog, literally and figuratively, in un-documented migrant labor in the present.

Westworld imagines the perfect technofuture, composed of bounded and technologically secure enclosures and based in the desires, prin-ciples, and ethos of the United States as an imperial power. The future is one of total surveillance and security, designed in the laboratory of a theme park. It is a place that combines Jean Baudrillard's Disney-land with William Bogard's simulation of surveillance. For the former, Disneyland is a simulation of society that supplants it as more real, as hyperreal, than the world beyond it.[12] Bogard notes in his early work that surveillance operates as a simulation that blurs the boundaries be-tween real and imagined to create new forms of control. He calls this the "imaginary of surveillant control" one that, like the hyperreal, seems more real than the social order it denotes.[13] The image or projection of control functions as control. Writing ten years later, Bogard revises this original notion and admits that he had given "too much weight" to the imaginary in the production of surveillance. In this later writing, he places more emphasis on the reality effect of the simulation, which "in-volves real and imperfect strategies of extending social control beyond systems of confinement, deterritorializing the space of enclosure, allow-ing closure to operate, as it were, 'at a distance,' or rather without regard to distance, the model of *telematic or virtual confinement*."[14] This diffu-sion of the boundary between real and actual surveillance, borderless surveillance, makes virtual the space of confinement. Such is the case in the Westworld theme park, in which the differentiation between inside and outside is deterritorialized, apparent in the diminishing boundary between human guest and robot host.

Westworld, based on the film of the same name (1973), offers a cynical view of the society of control as a laboratory and theme park for the lei-sure class. It is an example of the imaginary of surveillant control, which for Bogard is "a fantastic dream of seeing everything capable of being seen, recording every fact capable of being recorded, and accomplish-ing these things, whenever and wherever possible, prior to the event itself.["][15] This preemptive control, he notes, belongs in the realm of science fiction. Indeed, in this science-fiction imaginary, surveillance and control are so seamless that everything is not just seen and recorded but scripted, and any social friction or violence is planned, part of a design to ignite the pleasure and enjoyment of the elite visitor. The show exposes the obscene truth of a secured and closed system under total surveillance, its hierarchies of digital workers, exploited robotic labor, agents of enforcement, and the elite tourist class, forming the social composition of the future.

Surveillance in this world is aimed at stopping hosts from transgressing the deterritorialized border separating the park from the world beyond it, which is also the boundary separating human from host. This control is preemptive: hosts are programmed to lack consciousness of any division between reality and the park's story lines. In this world, the boundaries between actual and imagined surveillance dissolve. Control is perfected through the implantation of fabricated memories into preprogrammed narratives. The programmers and watchers, those who create and monitor this closed world, maintain their power as long as hosts remain unaware of their automated performance. The hosts participate in unchanging story worlds that function as laboratories of human desire, the outcomes of which yield data manipulable for various nefarious purposes. In a nightmarish reversal, the robots gain consciousness and agency and escape control by breaching the borders of their code and the park, escaping in search of the "world beyond," itself simply another virtual creation of the Delos corporation. The search for a "new world," articulated by the Native American host Akecheta, played by the Native actor Zahn McClarnon, is a catalyst for the collective mobilization of the hosts.[16]

As a vision or prefiguration of a just and liberatory future, the new world beyond the borders of Westworld promises freedom from subjugation, experienced in the closed circuit of ideology in the repetition of the same oppressive narratives and subsequent host objectification as forced labor in the theme park. The hosts cannot effect change within the current story lines; even the Mexican Revolution and its various factions are co-opted as a mere backdrop to the experience of the Old West. The social order of Westworld before the robot revolution is a form of border-security futurism, an example of the future imaginary and ideal of a bounded space with perfectly monitored borders under total surveillance and preemptively controlled. The robot revolution is an insurrection against this fantasy and future of total surveillance and control.

Other Futures

CBP border-security futurism, evinced in the principle of preemption—to "stop threats before they arrive at U.S. borders"—is reactive rather than creative. Moreover, it is destructive: the intensification of security might undo the border rather than reinforce it. The terrain and built environment are shaped by threat; the atmosphere of surveillance and countersurveillance creates a mood of unrest and elicits anxiety in the demand for unrelenting watchfulness and vigilance. For Sam Grabowska, the destruction of the US-Mexico border is inevitable, enacted by the shifting conditions and agents acting on it: "The overbearing and overcompensating strategies to protect inside from outside, self from other, end up eroding the functionality and proficiency of the border itself. The border begins to undo itself through anxiety."[17] The border regime is doomed to failure, energized and shaped by the dissolving forces of anxiety in a form of futurism that is ultimately destructive rather than creative.

For creative alternatives to border-security futurism, I turn to popular makers of various kinds—writers, designers, artists, activists, and thinkers—who imagine and design futures according to principles and goals of liberation from border imperialism or the border as a regime of global inequities. Joseph Nevins proposes a "right to the world," or fundamental right to move, as a way of rethinking the exclusions of nationalism and citizenship. He revises the notion, from Henri Lefebvre and later reconstrued by David Harvey, of the "right to the city," in which the city space is the site of negotiation of rights and democratic participation. Instead, Nevins asserts the right to the world, of mobility and at-will residence, as a human right. Article I of the Universal Declaration of Human Rights asserts that "all human beings are born free and equal in dignity and rights . . . and should act towards one another in a spirit of brotherhood."[18] The freedom of mobility includes equal access to the natural resources of the planet for all. Human rights are not rooted in localities, in cities or nation-states, but in the world. Nevins's vision of the future has a cosmopolitan ethic: "The struggle for a better world must also involve a right to a just share of the Earth's resources and to a homeland that is sustainable and secure in a broad sense—i.e. a right to stay home. Moreover, it must, especially for the globally disadvantaged, allow for the traversing of global space, the wandering of the paths on land and sea that connect and divide us."[19] This requires an imaginary in which borders are points of passage rather than barriers and secured zones.

This future orientation evokes what Natasha King calls a "no borders politics" that involves a refusal of nation-states and their attendant borders. Drawing on the work of Bridget Anderson, Nandita Sharma, and Cynthia Wright, she explores how no borders politics is an uncompromising call for abolition of the structures that divide and exclude. In this politics, migration is understood autonomously as outside a logic of security. Migration is a social fact and a human right, an activity that coalesces into a political movement outside state control. The continual assertion of the autonomy of migration builds a visible force of mobile peoples whose movement contests border regimes and creates a new social reality. Mediated forms of mobility and the right to move propagate a different imaginary about borders and migration.[20]

Lawrence Herzog, writing at the end of the last millennium, imagines the border not through the logic of security but as a laboratory of globalization, ethnic diversity, and cultural *mestizaje*, or mixing. The future borderlands, heralded by the signing of the North American Free Trade Agreement (NAFTA) in 1994, would yield a cultural amalgamation of North and South through a "collision" of landscape and architectural design styles: "We are headed directly into a new kind of collision—a collision of architecture and landscape. Our future is assigned an acronym—NAFTA—but what will it look like?"[21] In this scenario, NAFTA is a cardinal force, as a function of globalization, creating a border future evinced in the built environment. The border is a symptom of globalization and "a living experiment in the transcultural shaping of urban landscapes, a process that could spread over much of our planet in the next century."[22] The national frontier is a place to explore conflict, where the Global South collides with the Global North, in order to model future global cities.

For Michael Dear and Gustavo LeClerc, "art can change the future," and they imagine the shape of this future through trans-American cosmopolitan cities in a manner that links place with cultural production; these "postborder" cities are crucibles of innovation and the locus of forces of transformation. Dear and LeClerc imagine an aesthetic cartography of the "postborder city" as a generative origin and radical reconfiguration of future geopolitics. This future is accessible and effected through creative work by artists on both sides of the border, "engaged in creating new mental and material cartographies that proclaim our collective futures."[23] Likewise, Fernando Romero and the architectural design firm LAR designate the border as a site of potential binational development that models solutions to future global challenges: "We are hopeful that our study and vision will catalyze relations between two countries that share a problematic border, and that it will promote solidarity and equity among people rather than division and inequality. Through investigating the complex issues that surround the U.S.-Mexico border and its global implications today, we seek to exemplify the need for change and improvement in the future. In the interest of helping the generations of the future confront imminent challenges, it is our opinion that the development of these types of visions and alternatives are necessary."[24] The book-length project of these various designs, *Hyperborder*, argues for a border model that is comparative and emerges from a global context, much like border-security futurism, but does so in the service of a common vision for a future liberated from the exclusionary logic of border-security regimes. Instead, the border is a site of development, education, and infrastructure through the concept of the "hyperborder," or a site onto which to project various possible futures, a paradigmatic global arena for imagining a more equitable social order.

Hyperborder enumerates various possible future models, arguing that "tactics piloted along the U.S.-Mexico border that prove to positively influence the region's conditions could therefore potentially be utilized as models for the rest of the world."[25] Published in 2008, the book makes predictions for a future that have become the past. Some are cautionary and prescient. For example, the projected scenario of a sealed border in 2016 effects a devastating economic fallout and the United States' loss of esteem on the global stage. Others are adaptable policy suggestions for more just working conditions—for example, the creation of a system for precarious workers to qualify for Mexican-government pensions or the projection that employers will offer incentives for Mexican workers to migrate to the United States. In this border future, the borderlands are a privileged site and source of knowledge that promises much-sought-after higher-educational opportunities.

Hyperborder proposes urban formations in the borderlands that are granted binational status, thus decreasing undocumented migration, with travel permitted across the border-city space. This projection prefaces Fernando Romero's plans, created with the firm FR-EE, called Border City and presented in 2016.[26] The border city is a series of interlinked, hexagonally shaped hubs that extend outward across the borderlands joining the United States to Mexico. These binational plans and projections are based in actually existing and historically rooted economies and politics and are transformed to expand opportunities for both nations. While these plans are creative solutions to the conflict-ridden border, they reform the border logic to include more cooperation between the United States and Mexico. However, cooperation, as in the example of the World Border Security Congress or in the outcomes of NAFTA or the Border Industrialization Program, might yield more precarity for migrants and *maquiladora* workers in the borderlands by consolidating the border regime.

Cooperation to transform the border regime demands a critical orientation toward racial capitalism, or the role of racialization in the production of diminished social value. For instance, the cooperative agreement represented by NAFTA recast the colonial relationships of the Global North to the Global South; it privileged corporations over workers and the United States over Mexico in a manner that resulted in the reduction of wages, benefits, and protections for Mexican borderlands workers. The binational city creates shared space, yet the machinery of neoliberal capitalism, if not reconstrued, could derail plans for realignment of social, political, and national divisions. Steven Soderbergh's film *Traffic* (2000) imagines this vexed dynamic in the expedient shorthand of cinematic drama in a story line that promulgates an ideal of binational cooperation in the "War on Drugs" but ends with the subordination of the Mexican state, represented by the Tijuanense cop played by Benicio del Toro, to the US government.[27]

Figure 5.2. no-to-scale's *1954 Mile-Long Dining Table*, 2017. (https://no-to-scale.tumblr .com/; courtesy of no-to-scale)

The transborder city obviates the need for a wall, though it could be argued that it merely relocates barriers to the circumference of the binational city. Perhaps, rather than dispensing with the wall, it might be dialogically engaged as a public forum and space for the discussion of exclusionary politics.[28] The architectural firm no-to-scale redeploys the wall to imagine a different form of shared space. It turns the wall on its side to form a 1,954-mile-long dining table that unites peoples across nations through the hospitality of shared meals and conversation. The artistic renderings of the table illustrate people traveling from afar to participate in this binational social congress. A sign placed on the southern side of the dining table indicates its future orientation, aligned with Mexico, as the "Future site of the Mexico space port."[29] The border wall as table is a template and platform for the future, a public site and space for engaging with questions about cosmopolitan hospitality and freedom of mobility.

The project *1954 Mile-Long Dining Table* abstracts the borderlands from their current condition of militarization and surveillance and

Figure 5.3. "Future Site of the Mexico Space Port" sign at no-to-scale's *1954 Mile-Long Dining Table*, 2017. (https://no-to-scale.tumblr.com/; courtesy of no-to-scale)

re-visions them as a space of leisure and pleasure. These designs imagine forms of practical futures. Likewise, in 2019, the architectural design studio Rael San Fratello turned the actual border wall into a binational playground by placing three bright-pink teeter-totters in the metal slats of the wall. This event drew people from both sides who joined in the see-saw game. This design was first sketched by one of the founding members of Rael San Fratello, Ronald Rael, who created it as part of a number of models showcased in the anthology *Borderwall as Architecture*; it first appeared in his catalyst project "Borderwall Infrastructure." The latter re-makes the US-Mexico wall as the integration of water, renewable energy, and urban social infrastructure designed to benefit borderlands residents while remaining attentive to the ecological impact of this built environment. By engaging the border wall as architecture, Rael and the various contributors to his anthology—Teddy Cruz, Marcello Di Cintio, Norma Iglesias-Prieto, and Michael Dear—dialogically engage and deconstruct the social, political, and architectural barriers between the United States and Mexico. Rael dismantles walls through design, some that are drawn from actual efforts at migrant subversion and transgression of the wall—catapults, ramps, ladders, cannons, tunnels—and others that retool the wall through designs including pedestrian and bike paths, dams, water plants, parks, library, theaters, and solar-power farms.[30]

The various reconfigurations of the border wall might be described as a function of border design thinking. For Tony Fry and Eleni Kalantidou, this philosophy integrates Walter Mignolo's idea of border thinking with design theories in which the creation of spaces is accomplished through a critical reflection on coloniality in the Global South. They rethink borders and boundaries, both real and virtual, as future-oriented decolonial spaces. Mignolo's border philosophy erases the boundary between subject and object or knower and known to enable a way of thinking from the border or margins. While it is a way of thinking, it is nonetheless grounded in place and experience: "Border epistemology emerges from the experience, and the anger, of entanglement, border dwelling in power differential. Briefly, border thinking requires a shift in the geography of reasoning, a geopolitical conception of knowing, understanding and believing, a delinking from the assumption of modern and postmodern epistemology, hermeneutics and sensibility."[31] Border design thinking tackles the myriad problems arising from the calcification of borders during eras of increased global movement and migration. Fry and Kalantidou underscore the agency of design, "not as a grand vision of a global project" but as the "decision and direction" inherent to all things created and manufactured by humans. Designs embody direction, not as ends but as intentions toward some inherent goals.[32]

Border design thinking partakes in the conflicts of the present to creatively design toward a more equitable future. Rather than the sifting and sorting principles of border-security logic, design might encourage what Paul James calls "creative ontological friction" that "explicitly and reflexively recognizes ontological differences across different social formations."[33] This means catalyzing interactions across difference that encourage reflection on being "human in relation to other humans, objects, to nature and to categories of social being, including time, space, embodiment, epistemology and performativity."[34] The border future may not unfold in the territorial borderlands between nations, but it nonetheless explores intimacies among people, other animacies, and places that are real, fictional, and virtual.

While art and design create new spaces and built environments at the future border, borderlands science fiction builds worlds from the conditions of the present to critique and expose the wages of racial capitalism. Rosaura Sánchez and Beatrice Pita's novel *Lunar Braceros 2125–2148* and Alex Rivera's film *Sleep Dealer* (2008) caution of the future of work imagined by *Westworld*, where the dehumanization and disposability of the frontier worker is complete. In *Lunar Braceros 2125–2148*, disposable borderland workers are exiled to the final frontier zone of the moon. After their labors are terminated, their corporate overlords murder them rather than bear the cost obligation of their transport back to Earth. This scenario recalls that of *Sleep Dealer*, in which corporations desire the work without the workers and the various burdens represented by their physical presence.

Lunar Braceros 2125–2148 reimagines future frontiers along two related axes. The Earth colonizes the final frontier of the moon, while it realigns earthbound geopolitics in the creation of a binational territory through the new nation-state of Cali-Texas, which, akin to Romero's binational city, integrates former northern Mexican states (Tamaulipas, Coahuila, Chihuahua, Nuevo León, Sonora, and Baja California), former US southwestern states (Texas, Colorado, New Mexico, Arizona, Utah, California, and Nevada), and former US states in the Pacific Rim (Oregon, Washington, Alaska, and Hawaiʻi). This new alliance emerges from "transnational agri-business corporations and the four big biotechs, companies that controlled anything and everything that had to do with technology transfer, informatics and any kind of power generation, bio-fuel, nuclear or otherwise."[35] The geopolitical utopia of integration across the Global North and South promises to intensify the inequities of the current order and reveals the complete integration of surveillance capitalism with racial capitalism. Biotech companies are the new imperial overlords that exile Black and Brown workers to the lunar borderlands and eliminate them with impunity once they are no longer useful.

Westworld solves the problem of the irksome fleshy presence of workers by making them infinitely disposable and recyclable as human-like robots. In all three instances of this future life of the worker—*Sleep Dealer*, *Lunar Braceros*, and *Westworld*—a new consciousness emerges that allows workers to begin to resist their conditions of oppression and subjugation. *Westworld* allegorizes the emergence of this consciousness as robots begin to think for themselves, claim memories, and express and act on the desire for an alternate future, one different from that circumscribed by their enclosure and programming. These fictional worlds expose historical injustices to the marginalized by strategically flattening figurative language and literalizing metaphors about workers, who are treated not "as if" but *as* robots or disposable resources.

The future imaginaries of creative fictions expose what Dick Hebdige characterizes as the "virtual power of figurative language," particularly evident in the symbolic grammar of metaphor. Metaphors work as "time-bombs or viruses or seeds or sleepers which, if activated, disseminated, sown or woken up at the right time, will blow up, catch on, take root or spring into action some time in the future, some time after the moment of their enunciation."[36] Metaphors accomplish powerful rhetorical work that simplifies and accretes complicated realities under a single overdetermined signifier or set of signifiers. The caravan, a highly visible mobile force, is such a metaphor, one that circulates in public discourse as a sign of mass movement and political mobilization. We might be reminded of the powerful conclusion of Cheech Marin's *Born in East L.A.*, released in 1987 after the Immigration Reform and Control Act (IRCA) was signed into law in 1986, causing a split legal regime that enhanced the divide between documented and undocumented immigrants and resulted in increased INS raids and fomenting a rise in anti-immigrant sentiment. Public fears that tidal waves of immigrants were flooding the southern frontier garnered support for restrictive measures to "regain control of the border." In this post-IRCA story, Rudy, the main character, is a US citizen who is deported to Mexico in a mass deportation sweep and, after many attempts at returning to the United States, finally eyes success. In a final scene, he stands alone on the crest of a hill that slopes down into the United States. He raises his arms in a summoning gesture and is soon joined by a caravan of fellow travelers who outnumber the pair of agents patrolling the area. The scene ends dramatically with migrants moving en masse to descend the hill and traverse the border. They turn the phobic symbolic image of a "flood" or "wave" of immigrants into the liberatory politics of the caravan. The caravan forms what Michael Hardt and Antonio Negri describe as an "unusual kind of internationalist insurrection," one that, even if not articulated through the political, nonetheless constitutes "internationalist power" and an "insurrection against the border regimes of nation-states and the spatial hierarchies of the global system."[37]

Born in East L.A., through comedy, offers a vital and hopeful new vision of a mass movement of global proportions. It is prescient, if not exhortatory, of the politics of visibility of migrant caravans and mass mobilization reminiscent of the Day without an Immigrant strikes, ICE raid blockades, and the airport protests that followed the Muslim ban. These are all part of the same political caravan, a series of struggles that meet up and join forces to form a larger and more powerful movement. It reminds us, looking back, that imagined futures are not limited to genres of speculative fiction and might emanate from within the cultural archaeology of the borderlands. The caravan is both a symbol and a literal event of political mobilization, one that exposes the violence of border regimes and resists and displaces the abiding metaphors of the border as limit to dramatize the great power of the multitude and the incredible force of political visibility for social transformation.

ACKNOWLEDGMENTS

The writing of a book ends arbitrarily. It is never really complete but continues on in the relationships and common paths of thinking that formed along the way. I have many people to thank for being part of this process. I want to express my gratitude to the members of the Global South Lab and the Surveillance and Infrastructure research area of the Informatics Lab at the University of Virginia, particularly Liz Ellcessor, Natasha Heller, and Debjani Ganguly; to Debjani and the IHGC for creating a dynamic and intellectually nourishing space for scholars from all over the university and the world to come together. I thank Joshua Reeves for sharing his fascinating work with the Informatics Lab and for his intellectual generosity. I am indebted to Shoshana Magnet for her brilliance and for presenting her insightful research in the Labs. I thank Giulia Ricco and Renée Michelle Ragin, whose research group on the Global South and epistemologies of militarization has been generative of ongoing conversations and collaborative work. To the brilliant students of the Summer School in Global Theory at the University of Bologna who participated in the course on surveillance and borders, I owe a debt of gratitude. This work emerged from discussions with students of my border film and media courses throughout the years; I am truly grateful for their intellectual discourse. I gained so much from the artists and scholars at the Skidmore MDOCs forum on surveil/surveilled; I thank Sarah Friedland for the opportunity to participate in this spirited congress. I thank Christine Rüffert, Delia González de Reufels, Winifried Pauleit, and Angela Rabing of the International Bremen Film Conference for creating such a vibrant interdisciplinary space and for the opportunity to share this work with border film scholars and filmmakers. I thank Myra Washington, a wonderful scholar and host, for the opportunity to present aspects of this work at the University of New Mexico. Kent Ono has my gratitude for his generous, smart, and insightful feedback. Frederick Aldama has been truly supportive over the years, and I thank him for the opportunity to include my work in the many collections of work he has generated. I am indebted to José Carlos Villegas for his careful review and research assistance. Special thanks to no-to-scale for generous permission to use its artwork. I am grateful to the anonymous readers and to Eric Zinner, Dolma Ombadykow, and the series editors, Jonathan Gray, Aswin Punathambekar, and Adrienne Shaw, for helping to bring this project to fruition. For her luminous mind, her enduring care and support, I owe this and so much more to Dacia J. Harrold.

NOTES

INTRODUCTION

1. Moore et al., "Border Patrol Agent Is Dead in Texas."
2. Parks, "Stuff You Can Kick."
3. Andreas, *Border Games*, 9.
4. De Genova, *Working the Boundaries*, 242.
5. Inda, *Targeting Immigrants*, 140–141.
6. De León, *Land of Open Graves*.
7. See Fojas, *Border Bandits*.
8. Andreas, *Border Games*, 141.
9. Nail, "Violence at the Borders," 4.
10. Dunn, *Blockading the Border and Human Rights*.
11. Stumpf, "Crimmigration Crisis," 370–371.
12. Gandy, *Panoptic Sort*.
13. Lyon, *Surveillance Society*, 4. See also, Lyon, *Surveillance as Social Sorting*.
14. Zureik and Salter, introduction to *Global Surveillance and Policing*, 4.
15. G. Marx, "Some Conceptual Issues," 13.
16. Mezzadra and Neilson, *Border as Method*, viii.
17. Kittler, *Optical Media*, 225.
18. Ibid.
19. Burnham, *Rise of the Computer State*, 118.
20. Magnet, *When Biometrics Fail*, 125.
21. Gates, *Our Biometric Future*.
22. Haddal, "Border Security," 10–11.
23. See McCoy, *Policing America's Empire*.
24. Kaplan, *Aerial Aftermaths*.
25. Weizman, "Introduction to the Politics of Verticality."
26. Adey, *Aerial Life*, 2.
27. Walia, *Undoing Border Imperialism*, 5.
28. Martínez, *Troublesome Border*.
29. Paredes, *"With a Pistol in His Hand,"* xiv.
30. Limón, *American Encounters*, 3.
31. Gómez, *Revolutionary Imaginations of Greater Mexico*.
32. Camacho, *Migrant Imaginaries*, 2–3.
33. Acuña, *Occupied America*, vi.
34. See Barker, *Life of Stephen F. Austin*, 402.

35. Dunn, *Militarization of the U.S.-Mexico Border*, 9.
36. See Chavez, *Latino Threat*.
37. See Judith Butler on petty sovereigns, in *Precarious Life*.
38. Phelps, Bozeman, and Koenigsberg, "Comprehending the Polar Shift in Border Security Culture," 90–91.
39. Ibid., 98.
40. Moinester, "Beyond the Border and into the Heartland."
41. Buffett, *Our 50-State Border Crisis*.
42. US House of Representatives, *Arizona Border Surveillance Technology Plan*, 27.
43. Kalhan, "Immigration Surveillance," 55.
44. Lind, "Trump's Stripping of Passports from Some Texas Latinos."
45. Amoore and Hall, "Border Theatre."
46. Hall, *Transparent Traveler*.
47. Currah and Mulqueen, "Securitizing Gender."
48. American Civil Liberties Union, "Constitution in the 100-Mile Border Zone."
49. Miller, *Border Patrol Nation*, 12.
50. Rapiscan Systems, "People Screening."
51. Chomsky, *Undocumented*, 10.
52. Hernández, *Migra!*, 56.
53. Rak, *Border Patrol*, 2.
54. Ibid.
55. Ibid., 3.
56. Ibid., 4.
57. Ibid., 5.
58. Martinez, *Injustice Never Leaves You*.
59. Paredes, *"With a Pistol in His Hand,"* 23.
60. Ibid., 16.
61. Ngai, "Strange Career of the Illegal Alien."
62. De Genova, *Working the Boundaries*, 214–215.
63. Nevins. *Operation Gatekeeper*, 11.
64. Chomsky, *Undocumented*.
65. De Genova, *Working the Boundaries*, 215.
66. Kan, *Mexico's "Narco-Refugees,"* 16–17.
67. Ibid., 6.
68. Ibid., 26–27.
69. Ibid., 5.
70. Bebout, *Whiteness on the Border*.

CHAPTER 1: BORDERVEILLANT MEDIA

1. Scott, *Seeing like a State*, 1.
2. US Customs and Border Protection, *2012–2016 Border Patrol Strategic Plan*, 17.
3. See Reece Jones's *Border Walls* for a discussion of the dehumanizing phrasing of the "catch and release" policy (42).

4. US Department of Homeland Security, "Secure Border Initiative."
5. See Argueta, "Border Security."
6. US Department of Homeland Security, "'SBI*net* Program' Program Specific Recovery Act Plan," 1.
7. Ibid., 2.
8. Trevizo, "Border Patrol Pleased with New Tech Efforts," A01.
9. US Department of Homeland Security, "Testimony of Michael J. Fisher."
10. Lyon, Haggerty, and Ball, "Introducing Surveillance Studies," 2.
11. Tewksbury, "Crowdsourcing Homeland Security."
12. Grissom, "Border Watch Program Called Waste of Taxpayer Dollars."
13. BlueServo, "About Us."
14. Koselka, "Don't Mess with Texas!," 53.
15. American Civil Liberties Union, "Constitution in the 100-Mile Border Zone."
16. US Government Accountability Office, *Secure Border Initiative*.
17. See Fojas, *Border Bandits*.
18. Cavanaugh and Heilbrunn, "Behind the Scenes."
19. Ibid.
20. Dunn, *Militarization of the U.S.-Mexico Border*, 133–134.
21. Ibid., 134.
22. US Customs and Border Protection, "Border Patrol Tactical Unit (BORTAC)."
23. Miller, *Empire of Borders*, 4.
24. US Customs and Border Protection, "Border Patrol Tactical Unit (BORTAC)."
25. Andreas, *Border Games*, x.
26. Anderson, *Conquest of Texas*, 15.
27. Bauman, *Globalization*.
28. Alexander, *New Jim Crow*.
29. Norris and Armstrong, *Maximum Surveillance Society*, 67.
30. Ibid.
31. Hughes, "Governmentality, Blurred Boundaries, and Pleasure," 439.
32. Ouellette and Hay, *Better Living through Reality TV*, 2.
33. Reeves, *Citizen Spies*, 4.
34. Amar, *Security Archipelago*.
35. Dunn, *Militarization of the U.S.-Mexico Border*, 43–44.
36. Lyon, "9/11, Synopticon, and Scopophilia," 40.
37. See Fojas, *Border Bandits*.
38. Dorr, Elcioglu, and Gaydos, "Welcome to the Border."
39. Jones, "Border Wars."
40. G. Marx, "Tack in the Shoe and Taking Off the Shoe."
41. See Greene, "Drone Vision."
42. Border Film Project, home page.
43. Newell, Gomez, and Guajardo, "Information Seeking, Technology Use, and Vulnerability," 188.
44. Hennessy-Fiske, "Latest Migrant Tool of Resistance on the Border?"

45. Dominguez, "Border Research, Border Gestures," 1056.
46. Ibid.
47. American Civil Liberties Union, "Protecting Privacy from Aerial Surveillance."

CHAPTER 2: DRONE FUTURES
1. US Customs and Border Protection, *Vision and Strategy 2020*, 3.
2. Ibid., 20, 23.
3. Nixon, "Useful in War."
4. Wall and Monahan, "Surveillance and Violence from Afar," 240.
5. Martin, "Eye in the Sky," 01B.
6. Adams, "Laser-Shooting, Drone-Slaying Dune Buggy.
7. "US DHS Swamped," 1.
8. Martin and Steuter, *Drone Nation*, xi.
9. US Customs and Border Protection, "Concept of Operations," 63.
10. US Customs and Border Protection, *Office of Inspector General Review 2012*, 2.
11. Quoted in Chamayou, *Theory of the Drone*, 12.
12. Miller, "Border Patrol Capitalism."
13. Dunn, *Blockading the Border and Human Rights*.
14. Ibid., 59–61.
15. Ibid., 2.
16. Nevins, *Operation Gatekeeper*.
17. Dunn, *Militarization of the U.S.-Mexico Border*.
18. Dunn, *Blockading the Border and Human Rights*, 1–3.
19. Center for Immigration Studies, "Weaponization of Immigration," 6.
20. Ibid., 2.
21. US Customs and Border Protection, *2012–2016 Border Patrol Strategic Plan*, 4.
22. US Customs and Border Protection, *Vision and Strategy 2020*, 3.
23. Ibid., 10.
24. US Customs and Border Protection, "Concept of Operations," 63.
25. "Bot Flies."
26. Massumi, *Ontopower*, 6.
27. Ibid., 7.
28. Ibid., 10.
29. Quoted in Chamayou, *Theory of the Drone*, 62.
30. Mark, "Weaponized Wilderness," 4.
31. See Salter and Mutlu, "Psychoanalytic Theory and Border Security."
32. Klein, "Notes on Some Schizoid Mechanisms."
33. Heidegger, "Question Concerning Technology," 288.
34. Ibid.
35. Ibid., 309.
36. Heidegger, *Discourse on Thinking*, 51.
37. Ibid., 52.

38. Arendt, *Origins of Totalitarianism*.

39. Ibid., 56.

40. Dominguez, "Dronologies," 179–180.

41. Ibid., 191.

42. Porter, "Law Enforcement's Use of Weaponized Drone," 351.

43. Chamayou, *Theory of the Drone*, 13.

44. Sledge, "Senate Immigration Reform Proposal Backs Drones."

45. Peter, "Drones on the US Border."

46. Bataille, *Accursed Share*, 118.

47. Ibid., 122.

48. Jaffe, "Former Defense Secretary Gates Warns."

49. Derrida, *Death Penalty*, 48–49.

50. Benjamin, *Drone Warfare*, 8.

51. Derrida, *Death Penalty*, 22.

52. Mark, "Weaponized Wilderness," 4.

53. Bennet, "On Mexican Border," A06.

54. Stahl, *Militainment, Inc.*

55. Aldama, "Toward a Transfrontera-Latinx Aesthetic," 378.

56. Paulson, "Interview with Alex Rivera."

57. Quoted in Marez, *Farm Worker Futurism*, 1.

58. Aldama, "Toward a Transfrontera-Latinx Aesthetic," 377.

59. K. Marx, *Grundisse*, 140.

60. Fanon, *Black Skin, White Masks*.

61. See Fojas, *Migrant Labor and Border Securities in Pop Culture*.

62. Shaw, *Predator Empire*, 4.

63. American Civil Liberties Union, "Protecting Privacy from Aerial Surveillance," 1.

64. Greene, "Drone Vision."

65. Miller, "Border Patrol Capitalism," 152–153.

66. Ibid., 154–155.

67. Kingham, "Drones, Borders and Drugs," 2.

CHAPTER 3: WILD BORDER

1. Quoted on the book jacket of Abbey, *Beyond the Wall*.

2. Mueller, "Immigration Reform's Unintended Consequence."

3. W. Wright, *Wild West*, 3.

4. Christensen, "Wild West," 316.

5. Chris, *Watching Wildlife*, 11–12.

6. Callicot, "Contemporary Criticisms of the Received Wilderness Idea," 362.

7. Wilderness Act, Public Law 88-577 (16 USC 1131–1136), 88th Congress, 2nd session, September 3, 1964 (emphasis added).

8. Cronon, *Uncommon Ground*.

9. Nash, *Wilderness and the American Mind*, 3.

10. Ibid., xiii.
11. Ibid., 6.
12. Ibid., xiii.
13. Chief Luther Standing Bear, "Indian Wisdom," 201.
14. Nash, *Wilderness and the American Mind*, xiii–xiv.
15. Ibid., 1.
16. Wright, Dixon, and Thompson, *Fauna of the National Parks of the United States*, 94.
17. Ibid., 10.
18. Ibid.
19. Massé and Lunstrum, "Accumulation by Securitization."
20. Berger, "Why Look at Animals?"
21. Lippit, *Electric Animal*, 196.
22. Chris, *Watching Wildlife*, xiv.
23. Bousé, *Wildlife Films*, 9.
24. Ibid., 23–24.
25. Iraola, "Public Lands, Wilderness, and National Security," 792.
26. See Fojas, *Border Bandits*.
27. Singer, *Animal Liberation*, 119.
28. Quoted ibid., 7.
29. Heidegger, *Fundamental Concepts of Metaphysics*, 219.
30. Orwell, *Animal Farm*, 43.
31. Derrida, *Animal That Therefore I Am*, 4.
32. Ibid., 5.
33. Freccero, "Les Chats de Derrida," 154.
34. Orwell, *Animal Farm*, 139.
35. Quoted in Neocleous, *Universal Adversary*, 23–24.
36. Ibid., 24.
37. Ibid., 30.
38. Nevins, "Review of Jason de León's *The Land of Open Graves*," 102.
39. Aldama and Nericcio, *Talking #browntv*, 118.
40. Quoted in Iraola, "Public Lands, Wilderness, and National Security," 799.
41. Benson, *Wired Wilderness*, 2.
42. Rajchenberg and Héau-Lambert, "*Wilderness* vs. desierto?," 24.
43. Ibid.
44. Ibid., 25.
45. Ibid., 26.
46. Weber, *Myth and the History of the Hispanic Southwest*, 37.
47. Quoted ibid., 44.
48. R. Cox. *Environmental Communication and the Public Sphere*, 215.
49. The language of the border as "biological" and not "political" is that of the wildlife biologist Sergio Avila of the Sky Island Alliance, featured in *Wild versus Wall*.
50. Quoted in Roche et al., "Environmental Impacts of the Border Wall."

51. Shellabarger, Peterson, and Sills, "How Conservation and Humanitarian Groups Respond," 485.
52. L. Marx, *Machine in the Garden*, 5–6.

CHAPTER 4: IMPERIAL BORDER OPTICS
1. See Amoore *Politics of Possibility*.
2. Gates, "Globalization of Homeland Security."
3. Abdenebbi, "Passenger Data Exchange."
4. Woolley, "Border Force."
5. Virilio, *Lost Dimension*, 10.
6. Adey, "Airports, Mobility and the Calculative Architecture," 438.
7. Parkes, "Strangest Thing."
8. McCarthy, "Untapped Revenue," 38.
9. Quoted in Keung, "Border Security Reality Show."
10. Quoted ibid.
11. Ibid.
12. Richelson and Ball, *Ties That Bind*, 2–3.
13. Mattelart, *Globalization of Surveillance*, 60.
14. Richelson, *US Intelligence Community*, 376.
15. J. Cox, "Canada and the Five Eyes Intelligence Community," cited in O'Neil, "Australia and the 'Five Eyes' Intelligence Network," 536.
16. Bowling and Sheptycki, "Global Policing, Mobility and Social Control," 67.
17. Weissman, *Transnational Television Drama*, 6–7.
18. Havens, "Exhibiting Global Television."
19. Andrejevic, "'Securitainment' in the Post-9/11 Era."
20. Quoted in Hughes. "Governmentality, Blurred Boundaries, and Pleasure," 439.
21. Ibid., 440.
22. Pearson, "New Zealand Reality Television," 124.
23. Hall, *Transparent Traveler*.
24. Massumi quoted in Amoore, *Politics of Possibility*, 2–3.
25. Aaltola, "International Airport," 261–262.
26. Auge, *Non-places*, 96.
27. Certeau, *Practice of Everyday Life*.
28. Auge, *Non-places*, 111.
29. Ibid., 103.
30. Adey, "Airports, Mobility and the Calculative Architecture."
31. Gordon, *Naked Airport*, 43–44.
32. Burnett, "PR and the Selling of Border Controls."
33. Cited in Price and Nethery, "Truth-Telling at the Border," 151–152.
34. Adey, "Borders, Identification and Surveillance," 196.
35. On the history of the passport as it relates to the transformation of the surveillance regime, see Robertson, *Passport in America*.
36. Moore and Currah, "Legally Sexed," 59.

37. Price and Nethery, "Truth-Telling at the Border," 150.
38. Quoted in Price and Nethery, "Truth-Telling at the Border," 149.

CHAPTER 5: BORDER FUTURES

1. Martin, "Eye in the Sky," 01B.
2. Adey, "Borders, Identification and Surveillance," 193.
3. Montfort, *Future*, 4.
4. See Albert, *Practical Utopia*; E. Wright, "Socialism and Real Utopias," 75.
5. Walia, *Undoing Border Imperialism*, 11.
6. Kelley, *Freedom Dreams*, xii.
7. Toffler, *Future Shock*, 469.
8. Dublin, *Futurehype*, 130.
9. Ibid., 160.
10. US Customs and Border Protection, *CBP Strategy 2020–2025*, 4.
11. Ibid., 7.
12. Baudrillard, *Simulacra and Simulation*.
13. Bogard, *Simulation of Surveillance*, 4.
14. Bogard, "Welcome to the Society of Control," 71.
15. Bogard, *Simulation of Surveillance*, 4.
16. Kelley, *Freedom Dreams*, 3.
17. Grabowska, "Anxious Architecture," 115.
18. Quoted in Nevins, "Right to the World," 1351.
19. Ibid., 1359.
20. King, *No Borders*.
21. Herzog, *From Aztec to High Tech*, x.
22. Ibid., xi.
23. Dear and LeClerc, preface to *Postborder City*, xi; Dear and LeClerc, introduction to *Postborder City*, 1.
24. Fernando Romero and LAR, *Hyperborder*, 17.
25. Ibid., 16.
26. FR-EE, "Border City."
27. See Fojas, *Border Bandits*.
28. See Cruz, "Border Wall as Public Space?"
29. no-to-scale, "1954 Mile-Long Dining Table."
30. Rael, *Borderwall as Architecture*.
31. Fry and Kalantidou, "Exchange," 174.
32. Fry and Kalantidou, "Design in the Borderlands," 1.
33. James, "Urban Design for the Global South," 93.
34. Ibid.
35. Sánchez and Pita, *Lunar Braceros*, 6–7.
36. Hebdige, "Training Some Thoughts on the Future," 274.
37. Hardt and Negri, "Empire, Twenty Years On," 77.

BIBLIOGRAPHY

Aaltola, Mika. "The International Airport: The Hub and Spoke Pedagogy of the American Empire." *Global Networks* 5, no. 3 (2005): 261–278.

Abbey, Edward. *Beyond the Wall: Essays from the Outside*. New York: Holt, Rinehart and Winston, 1984.

Abdenebbi, Nariess. "Passenger Data Exchange: API and PNR." Paper presented at the ICAO, World Border Security Congress, Madrid, Spain, 2018.

Acuña, Rudolfo. *Occupied America: A History of Chicanos*. New York: Harper and Row, 1988.

Adams, Eric. "Humanity Gets a Laser-Shooting, Drone-Slaying Dune Buggy." *Wired*, October 11, 2017.

Adey, Peter. *Aerial Life: Spaces, Mobilities, Affects*. West Sussex, UK: Wiley-Blackwell, 2010.

———. "Airports, Mobility and the Calculative Architecture of Affective Control." *Geoforum* 39 (2008): 438–451.

———. "Borders, Identification and Surveillance: New Regimes of Border Control." In *Routledge Handbook of Surveillance Studies*, edited by Kirstie Ball, Kevin D. Haggerty, and David Lyon, 193–200. London: Routledge, 2012.

Albert, Michael. *Practical Utopia: Strategies for a Desirable Society*. New York: PM, 2017.

Aldama, Frederick. "Toward a Transfrontera-Latinx Aesthetic: An Interview with Filmmaker Alex Rivera." *Latino Studies* 15 (2017): 373–380.

Aldama, Frederick, and William Nericcio. *Talking #browntv: Latinas and Latinos on the Screen*. Columbus: Ohio State University Press, 2019.

Alexander, Michelle. *The New Jim Crow: Mass Incarceration in the Age of Colorblindness*. New York: New Press, 2010.

Amar, Paul. *The Security Archipelago: Human-Security States, Sexual Politics, and the End of Neoliberalism*. Durham, NC: Duke University Press, 2013.

American Civil Liberties Union. "The Constitution in the 100-Mile Border Zone." Accessed September 17, 2019. www.aclu.org.

———. "Protecting Privacy from Aerial Surveillance: Recommendations for Government Use of Drone Aircraft." December 2011. www.aclu.org.

Amoore, Louise. *The Politics of Possibility: Risk and Security beyond Probability*. Durham, NC: Duke University Press, 2013.

Amoore, Louise, and Alexandra Hall. "Border Theatre: On the Arts of Security and Resistance." *Cultural Geographies* 17, no. 3 (2010): 299–319.

Anderson, Gary Clayton. *The Conquest of Texas: Ethnic Cleansing in the Promised Land, 1820–1875*. Norman: University of Oklahoma Press, 2005.

Andreas, Peter. *Border Games*. Ithaca, NY: Cornell University Press, 2000.

Andrejevic, Mark. "'Securitainment' in the Post-9/11 Era." *Continuum: Journal of Media and Cultural Studies* 25, no. 2 (2011): 165–175.

Arendt, Hannah. *The Origins of Totalitarianism*. New York: World, 1964.

Argueta, Carla N. "Border Security: Immigration Enforcement between Ports of Entry." Congressional Research Service, April 19, 2016.

Auge, Marc. *Non-places: Introduction to an Anthropology of Supermodernity*. Translated by John Howe. New York: Verso, 1995.

Barker, Eugene. *The Life of Stephen F. Austin, Founder of Texas, 1793–1836*. Austin: University of Texas Press, 1969.

Bataille, Georges. *The Accursed Share: An Essay on General Economy*. New York: Zone Books, 1988.

Baudrillard, Jean. *Simulacra and Simulation*. Translated by Sheila Faria Glaser. Ann Arbor: University of Michigan Press, 1994.

Bauman, Zygmunt. *Globalization: The Human Consequences*. Oxford, UK: Polity, 1998.

Bebout, Lee. *Whiteness on the Border: Mapping the U.S. Racial Imagination in Brown and White*. New York: NYU Press, 2016.

Benjamin, Medea. *Drone Warfare: Killing by Remote Control*. New York: Verso, 2013.

Bennet, Brian. "On Mexican Border, Drones Have Not Proved Their Worth." *Washington Post*, May 6, 2012.

Benson, Etienne. *Wired Wilderness: Technologies of Tracking and the Making of Modern Wildlife*. Baltimore: John Hopkins University Press, 2010.

Berger, John. "Why Look at Animals?" In *Selected Essays of John Berger*, edited by Geoff Dyer, 259–273. New York: Vintage Books, 2003.

BlueServo. "About Us." Accessed August 12, 2019. www.blueservco.com.

Bogard, William. *The Simulation of Surveillance: Hypercontrol in Telematic Societies*. New York: Cambridge University Press, 1996.

———. "Welcome to the Society of Control: The Simulation of Surveillance Revisited." In *The New Politics of Surveillance and Visibility*, edited by Kevin D. Haggerty and Richard V. Ericson, 55–78. Toronto: University of Toronto Press, 2006.

Border Film Project. Home page. Accessed May 17, 2018. www.borderfilmproject.com.

"Bot Flies." *Economist*, December 16, 2017, 71–72.

Bousé, Derek. *Wildlife Films*. Philadelphia: University of Pennsylvania Press, 2000.

Bowling, Ben, and James Sheptycki. "Global Policing, Mobility and Social Control." In *The Routledge Handbook on Crime and International Migration*, edited by Sharon Pickering and Julie Ham, 57–74. New York: Routledge, 2015.

Buffett, Howard G. *Our 50-State Border Crisis: How the Mexican Border Fuels the Drug Epidemic across America*. New York: Hachette Books, 2018.

Burnett, Jon. "PR and the Selling of Border Controls." Institute of Race Relations, May 21, 2019.

Burnham, David. *The Rise of the Computer State*. New York: Random House, 1983.

Butler, Judith. *Precarious Life: The Powers of Mourning and Violence*. New York: Verso, 2004.

Callicot, J. Baird. "Contemporary Criticisms of the Received Wilderness Idea." In *The Wilderness Debate Rages On: Continuing the Great New Wilderness Debate*, edited by Michael P. Nelson and J. Baird Callicot, 355–377. Athens: University of Georgia Press, 2008.

Camacho, Alicia Schmidt. *Migrant Imaginaries: Latino Cultural Politics in the U.S.-Mexico Borderlands*. New York: NYU Press, 2008.

Cavanaugh, Maureen, and Sharon Heilbrunn "Behind the Scenes of National Geographic's *Border Wars* Documentary." KPBS Public Broadcasting, January 5, 2010.

Center for Immigration Studies. "Weaponization of Immigration." February 8, 2008. http://cis.org.

Certeau, Michel de. *The Practice of Everyday Life*. Translated by Steven F. Rendall. Berkeley: University of California Press, 1988.

Chamayou, Gregoire. *A Theory of the Drone*. Translated by Janet Lloyd. New York: New Press, 2013.

Chavez, Leo. *The Latino Threat: Constructing Immigrants, Citizens and the Nation*. Stanford, CA: Stanford University Press, 2008.

Chief Luther Standing Bear. "Indian Wisdom." In *The Great New Wilderness Debate*, edited by J. Baird Callicot and Michael P. Nelson, 201–206. Athens: University of Georgia Press, 1998.

Chomsky, Aviva. *Undocumented: How Immigration Became Illegal*. Boston: Beacon, 2014.

Chris, Cynthia. *Watching Wildlife*. Minneapolis: University of Minnesota Press, 2006.

Christensen, Paul. "The 'Wild West': The Life and Death of a Myth." *Southwest Review* 93, no. 3 (2008): 310–325.

Cox, James. "Canada and the Five Eyes Intelligence Community." Canadian Defence and Foreign Affairs Institute Working Group Papers, December 2012.

Cox, Robert. *Environmental Communication and the Public Sphere*. Los Angeles: Sage, 2013.

Cronon, William *Uncommon Ground: Rethinking the Human Place in Nature*. New York: Norton, 1996.

Cruz, Teddy. "Border Wall as Public Space?" In *Borderwall as Architecture: A Manifesto for the U.S.-Mexico Boundary*, edited by Ronald Rael, vii–xiv. Berkeley: University of California Press, 2017.

Currah, Paisley, and Tara Mulqueen. "Securitizing Gender: Identity, Biometrics, and Transgender Bodies at the Airport." *Social Research: An International Quarterly* 78, no. 2 (2011): 557–582.

Dear, Michael, and Gustavo LeClerc. Introduction to *Postborder City: Cultural Spaces of Bajalta California*, edited by Michael Dear and Gustavo LeClerc, 1–30. New York: Routledge, 2003.

———. Preface to *Postborder City: Cultural Spaces of Bajalta California*, edited by Michael Dear and Gustavo LeClerc, xi–xiv. New York: Routledge, 2003.

De Genova, Nicholas. *Working the Boundaries: Race, Space, and "Illegality" in Mexican Chicago*. Durham, NC: Duke University Press, 2005.

De León, Jason. *The Land of Open Graves: Living and Dying on the Migrant Trail*. Oakland: University of California Press, 2015.

Derrida, Jacques. *The Animal That Therefore I Am*. Translated by David Wills. New York: Fordham University Press, 2008.

———. *The Death Penalty*. Vol. 1. Translated by Peggy Kamuf. Chicago: University of Chicago, 2013.

Dominguez, Ricardo. "Border Research, Border Gestures: The Transborder Immigrant Tool." *American Quarterly* 71, no. 4 (2019): 1053–1058.

———. "Dronologies: Or Twice-Told Tales." In *Life in the Age of Drone Warfare*, edited by Lisa Parks and Caren Kaplan, 178–194. Durham, NC: Duke University Press, 2017.

Dorr, Noam, Emine Fidan Elcioglu, and Lindsey Gaydos. "'Welcome to the Border': National Geographic's *Border Wars* and the Naturalization of Border Militarization." *WorkingUSA: The Journal of Labor and Society* 7 (2014): 45–60.

Dublin, Max. *Futurehype: The Tyranny of Prophecy*. New York: Penguin Books, 1990.

Dunn, Timothy. *Blockading the Border and Human Rights*. Austin: University of Texas Press, 2009.

———. *The Militarization of the U.S.-Mexico Border, 1978–1992: Low Intensity Conflict Doctrine Comes Home*. Austin: University of Texas Press, 1996.

Fanon, Frantz. *Black Skin, White Masks*. Translated by Richard Philcox. New York: Grove, 2008.

Fojas, Camilla. *Border Bandits: Hollywood on the Southern Frontier*. Austin: University of Texas Press, 2008.

———. *Migrant Labor and Border Securities in Pop Culture*. New York: Routledge, 2017.

Freccero, Carla. "Les Chats de Derrida." In *Derrida and Queer Theory*, edited by Christian Hite, 132–163. Goleta, CA: Punctum Books, 2017.

FR-EE. "Border City." Accessed April 1, 2020. www.fr-ee.org.

Fry, Tony, and Eleni Kalantidou. "Design in the Borderlands: An Introduction." In *Design in the Borderlands*, edited by Eleni Kalantidou and Tony Fry, 1–11. London: Routledge, 2014.

———. "An Exchange: Questions from Tony Fry and Eleni Kalantidou and answers from Walter Mignolo." In *Design in the Borderlands*, edited by Eleni Kalantidou and Tony Fry, 173–188. London: Routledge, 2014.

Gandy, Oscar. *The Panoptic Sort*. Boulder, CO: Westview, 1993.

Gates, Kelly. "The Globalization of Homeland Security." In *Routledge Handbook of Surveillance Studies*, edited by Kirstie Ball, Kevin D. Haggerty, and David Lyon, 292–299. London: Routledge, 2012.

———. *Our Biometric Future: Facial Recognition Technology and the Culture of Surveillance*. New York: NYU Press, 2011.

Gómez, Alan Eladio. *The Revolutionary Imaginations of Greater Mexico: Chicana/o Radicalism, Solidarity Politics, and Latin American Social Movements*. Austin: University of Texas Press, 2016.

Gordon, Alastair. *Naked Airport: A Cultural History of the World's Most Revolutionary Structure*. New York: Metropolitan Books, 2004.

Grabowska, Sam. "Anxious Architecture: Sleep, Anxiety, and Death in the U.S.-Mexico Borderlands." *Footprint: Delft School of Design Journal* 10, no. 2 (2016): 115–136.

Greene, Daniel. "Drone Vision." *Surveillance and Society* 13, no. 2 (2015): 233–249.

Grissom, Brandi. "Border Watch Program Called Waste of Taxpayer Dollars." *El Paso Times*, November 25, 2008.

Haddal, Chad. "Border Security: The Role of the U.S. Border Patrol." Congressional Research Service Report, August 11, 2010.

Hall, Rachel. *The Transparent Traveler: The Performance and Culture of Airport Security*. Durham, NC: Duke University Press, 2015.

Hardt, Michael, and Antonio Negri. "Empire, Twenty Years On." *New Left Review* 120 (2019): 67–92.

Havens, Timothy J. "Exhibiting Global Television: On the Business and Cultural Functions of Global Television Fairs." *Journal of Broadcasting and Electronic Media* 47, no. 1 (2003): 18–35.

Hebdige, Dick. "Training Some Thoughts on the Future." In *Mapping the Futures: Local Cultures, Global Change*, edited by Jon Bird, Barry Curtis, Tim Putman, George Robertson, and Lisa Tickner, 270–279. London: Routledge, 1993.

Heidegger, Martin. *Discourse on Thinking*. New York: Harper and Row, 1966.

———. *The Fundamental Concepts of Metaphysics: World, Finitude, Solitude*. Translated by William McNeil and Nicholas Walker. Bloomington: Indiana University Press, 1995.

———. "The Question Concerning Technology." In *Basic Writings*, edited by David Krell, 283–317. New York: Harper and Row, 1977.

Hennessy-Fiske, Molly. "The Latest Migrant Tool of Resistance on the Border? A Video App." *Los Angeles Times*, June 3, 2018.

Hernández, Kelly Lytle. *Migra! A History of the U.S. Border Patrol*. Berkeley: University of California Press, 2010.

Herzog, Lawrence. *From Aztec to High Tech: Architecture and Landscape across the Mexico-United States Border*. Baltimore: Johns Hopkins University Press, 1999.

Hughes, Peter. "Governmentality, Blurred Boundaries, and Pleasure in the Docusoap *Border Security*." *Continuum: Journal of Media and Cultural Studies* 24, no. 3 (2010): 439–449.

Inda, Jonathan. *Targeting Immigrants: Government, Technology, and Ethics*. Malden, MA: Blackwell, 2006.

Iraola, Roberto. "Public Lands, Wilderness, and National Security." *Penn State Law Review* 109, no. 3 (2005): 791–813.

Jaffe, Greg. "Former Defense Secretary Gates Warns against Lure of Drone Warfare." *Washington Post*, October 23, 2013. www.washingtonpost.com.

James, Paul. "Urban Design for the Global South: Ontological Design in Practice." In *Design in the Borderlands*, edited by Eleni Kalantidou and Tony Fry, 91–108. London: Routledge, 2014.

Jones, Reese. *Border Walls: Security and the War on Terror in the United States, India, and Israel*. London: Zed Books, 2012.

———. "Border Wars: Narratives and Images of the U.S.-Mexico Border on TV." *Acme: An International E-Journal for Critical Geographies* 13, no. 3 (2014): 530–550.

Kalhan, Anil. "Immigration Surveillance." *Maryland Law Review* 74, no. 1 (2014): 1–78.

Kan, Paul Rexton. *Mexico's "Narco-Refugees": The Looming Challenge for U.S. National Security*. Carlisle, PA: Strategic Studies Institute, US Army War College, 2011.

Kaplan, Caren, *Aerial Aftermaths: Wartime from Above*. Durham, NC: Duke University Press, 2018.

Kelley, Robin D. G. *Freedom Dreams: The Black Radical Imagination*. Boston: Beacon, 2002.

Keung, Nicholas. "Border Security Reality Show Called Risk for Vulnerable Migrants." *Star*, April 30, 2013. http://thestar.com.

King, Natasha. *No Borders: The Politics of Immigration Control and Resistance*. London: Zed Books, 2016.

Kingham, Tony. "Drones, Borders and Drugs." *Border Security Report* 11, no. 2 (2018): 2.

Kittler, Friedrich. *Optical Media: Berlin Lectures 1999*. Translated by Anthony Enns. Cambridge, UK: Polity, 2002.

Klein, Melanie. "Notes on Some Schizoid Mechanisms." *International Journal of Psychoanalysis* 27 (1946): 99–110.

Koselka, Hille. "'Don't Mess with Texas!': *Texas Virtual Border Watch Program* and the (Botched) Politics of Responsibilization." *Crime Media Culture* 7, no. 1 (2011): 49–65.

Limón, José. *American Encounters: Greater Mexico, the United States, and the Erotics of Culture*. Boston: Beacon, 1998.

Lind, Dara. "Trump's Stripping of Passports from some Texas Latinos, Explained." *Vox*, August 30, 2018. www.vox.com.

Lippit, Akira Mizuta. *Electric Animal: Toward a Rhetoric of Wildlife*. Minneapolis: University of Minnesota Press, 2000.

Lyon, David. "9/11, Synopticon, and Scopophilia: Watching and Being Watched." In *The New Politics of Surveillance and Visibility*, edited by Kevin D. Haggerty and Richard Ericson, 35–54. Toronto: University of Toronto Press, 2006.

———. *Surveillance as Social Sorting*. London: Routledge, 2003.

———. *Surveillance Society: Monitoring Everyday Life*. Buckingham, UK: Open University Press, 2001.

Lyon, David, Kevin Haggerty, and Kirstie Ball. "Introducing Surveillance Studies." In *Handbook of Surveillance Studies*, edited by David Lyon, Kevin Haggerty, and Kirstie Ball, 1–11. New York: Routledge, 2012.

Magnet, Shoshanna. *When Biometrics Fail: Gender, Race, and the Technology of Identity*. Durham, NC: Duke University Press, 2011.

Marez, Curtis. *Farm Worker Futurism: Speculative Technologies of Resistance*. Minneapolis: University of Minnesota Press, 2016.

Mark, Jason. "Weaponized Wilderness." *Sierra*, September–October 2017, 4.

Martin, Gary. "Eye in the Sky Takes Its First Look at Area along the U.S.-Mexico Border." *San Antonio Express News*, June 5, 2010.

Martin, Geoff, and Erin Steuter. *Drone Nation: The Political Economy of America's New Way of War*. Lanham, MD: Lexington Books, 2017.

Martìnez, Mònica Muñoz. *The Injustice Never Leaves You: Anti-Mexican Violence in Texas*. Cambridge, MA: Harvard University Press, 2018.

Martínez, Oscar. *Troublesome Border*. Tucson: Arizona University Press, 2006.

Marx, Gary T. "Some Conceptual Issues in the Study of Borders and Surveillance." In *Global Surveillance and Policing: Borders, Security, Identity*, edited by Elia Zureik and Mark B. Salter, 11–35. Devon, UK: Willan, 2005.

———. "A Tack in the Shoe and Taking Off the Shoe: Neutralization and Counterneutralization Dynamics." *Surveillance and Society* 6, no. 3 (2009): 294–306.

Marx, Karl. *The Grundisse*. Edited by David McLellan. New York: Harper and Row, 1971.

Marx, Leo. *The Machine in the Garden: Technology and the Pastoral Ideal in America*. New York: Oxford University Press, 2000.

Massé, Francis, and Elizabeth Lunstrum. "Accumulation by Securitization: Commercial Poaching, Neoliberal Conservation, and the Creation of New Wildlife Frontiers." *Geoforum* 69 (2016): 227–237.

Massumi, Brian. *Ontopower: War, Powers, and the State of Perception*. Durham, NC: Duke University Press, 2015.

Mattelart, Armand. *The Globalization of Surveillance*. Translated by Susan Taponier and James A. Cohen. Cambridge, UK: Polity, 2010.

McCarthy, Gerry. "Untapped Revenue—The Critics: Television." *Sunday Times*, September 21, 2008.

McCoy, Alfred. *Policing America's Empire*. Madison: University of Wisconsin Press, 2009.

Mezzadra, Sandro, and Brett Neilson. *Border as Method, or the Multiplication of Labor*. Durham, NC: Duke University Press, 2013.

Miller, Todd. "Border Patrol Capitalism." *NACLA Report on the Americas* 48, no. 2 (2016).

———. *Border Patrol Nation: Dispatches from the Front Lines of Homeland Security*. San Francisco: City Lights Books, 2014.

———. *Empire of Borders: The Expansion of the U.S. Border around the World*. New York: Verso, 2019.

Moinester, Margot. "Beyond the Border and Into the Heartland: Spatial Patterning of U.S. Immigration Detention." *Demography* 55 (2018): 1147–1193.

Montfort, Nick. *The Future*. Cambridge, MA: MIT Press, 2017.

Moore, Lisa Jean, and Paisley Currah. "Legally Sexed: Birth Certificates and Transgender Citizens." In *Feminist Surveillance Studies*, edited by Rachel E. Dubrofsky and Shoshana Amielle Magnet, 58–76. Durham, NC: Duke University Press, 2015.

Moore, Robert, Lindsey Bever, Derek Hawkins, and Nick Miroff. "A Border Patrol Agent Is Dead in Texas, but the Circumstances Remain Murky." *Washington Post*, November 20, 2017.

Mueller, Deena. "Immigration Reform's Unintended Consequence: Providing Greater Justification for Border Patrol to Waive Environmental Compliance at the U.S.-Mexico Border." *William and Mary Environmental Law and Policy Review* 37 (2013): 785–812.

Nail, Thomas. "Violence at the Borders: Nomadic Solidarity and Non-status Migrant Resistance." *Radical Philosophy Review* 15, no. 1 (2012): 1–12.

Nash, Roderick. *Wilderness and the American Mind*. New Haven, CT: Yale University Press, 1982.

Neocleous, Mark. *The Universal Adversary: Security, Capital and "The Enemies of All Mankind."* New York: Routledge, 2016.

Nevins, Joseph. *Operation Gatekeeper: The Rise of the "Illegal Alien" and the Making of the U.S.-Mexico Boundary*. New York: Routledge, 2002.

———. "Review of Jason de León's *The Land of Open Graves: Living and Dying on the Migrant Trail*." *NACLA Report on the Americas* 48, no. 1 (2016): 101–102.

———. "The Right to the World." *Antipode* 49, no. 5 (2017): 1349–1367.

Newell, Bryce Clayton, Ricardo Gomez, and Verónica E. Guajardo. "Information Seeking, Technology Use, and Vulnerability among Migrants at the United States–Mexico Border." *Information Society* 32, no. 3 (2016): 176–191.

Ngai, Mai. "The Strange Career of the Illegal Alien: Immigration Restriction and Deportation Policy in the United States, 1921–1965." *Law and History Review* 21, no. 1 (2003): 69–107.

Nixon, Ron. "Though Useful in War, Drones May Be Too Costly for Use along U.S. Borders." *New York Times*, November 3, 2016, A15(L).

Norris, Clive, and Gary Armstrong. *The Maximum Surveillance Society: The Rise of CCTV*. Oxford, UK: Berg, 1999.

no-to-scale. "1954 Mile-Long Dining Table." Tumblr, September 12, 2017. https://no-to-scale.tumblr.com.

O'Neil, Andrew. "Australia and the 'Five Eyes' Intelligence Network: The Perils of an Asymmetric Alliance." *Australian Journal of International Affairs* 71, no. 5 (2017): 529–543.

Orwell, George. *Animal Farm*. New York: Penguin Books, 1996.

Ouellette, Laurie, and James Hay. *Better Living through Reality TV: Television and Post-welfare Citizenship*. Malden, MA: Blackwell, 2008.

Paredes, Américo. *"With a Pistol in His Hand": A Border Ballad and Its Hero*. Austin: University of Texas Press, 1958.

Parkes, Melenie. "The Strangest Thing . . ." Stuff.co.nz, September 12, 2019.

Parks, Lisa. "'Stuff You Can Kick': Toward a Theory of Media Infrastructures." In *Humanities and the Digital*, edited by Patrik Svensson and David Theo Goldberg, 355–373. Cambridge, MA: MIT Press, 2015.

Paulson, Steve. "Interview with Alex Rivera." National Public Radio, August 10, 2014.

Pearson, Sarina. "New Zealand Reality Television: Hostile or Hospitable?" In *Ecomedia: Key Issues*, edited by Stephen Rust, Salma Monani and Sean Cubitt, 118–140. New York: Routledge, 2016.

Peter, Tom. "Drones on the US Border: Are They Worth the Price?" *Christian Science Monitor*, February 5, 2014.

Phelps, James, J. Michael Bozeman, and Monica Koenigsberg. "Comprehending the Polar Shift in Border Security Culture: Restoring Effective Sovereignty." In *Homeland Security Cultures: Enhancing Values While Fostering Resilience*, edited by Alexander Siedschlag and Andrea Jerkovic, 79–102. Lanham, MD: Rowman and Littlefield, 2018.

Porter, Amanda. "Law Enforcement's Use of Weaponized Drones: Today and Tomorrow." *Saint Louis University Law Journal* 61, no. 2 (2017): 351–370.

Price, Emma, and Amy Nethery. "Truth-Telling at the Border: An Audience Appraisal of *Border Security*." *Media International Australia* 142 (212): 148–156.

Rael, Ronald, ed. *Borderwall as Architecture: A Manifesto for the U.S.-Mexico Boundary*. Berkeley: University of California Press, 2017.

Rajchenberg, S. Enrique, and Catherine Héau-Lambert. "*Wilderness* vs. desierto? Representaciones del septentrión mexicano en el siglo XIX." *Norteamérica* 4, no. 2 (2009): 15–36.

Rak, Mary Kidder. *Border Patrol*. Boston: Houghton Mifflin, 1938.

Rapiscan Systems. "People Screening." Accessed September 10, 2019. www.rapiscansystems.com.

Reeves, Joshua. *Citizen Spies: The Long Rise of America's Surveillance Society*. New York: NYU Press, 2017.

Richelson, Jeffrey T. *The US Intelligence Community*. Boulder, CO: Westview, 2016.

Richelson, Jeffrey T., and Desmond Ball. *The Ties That Bind: Intelligence Cooperation between the UKUSA Countries—The United Kingdom, the United States of America, Canada, Australia and New Zealand*. Boston: Allen and Unwin, 1985.

Robertson, Craig. *The Passport in America: The History of a Document*. New York: Oxford University Press, 2010.

Roche, David, Dan Millis, Any Gordon, Sarah Krakoff, and Sarah Burt. "Environmental Impacts of the Border Wall." Environmental Law Institute, Washington, DC, 2017.

Romero, Fernando, and LAR. *Hyperborder: The Contemporary U.S.-Mexico Border and Its Future*. New York: Princeton Architectural Press, 2008.

Salter, Mark B., and Can E. Mutlu. "Psychoanalytic Theory and Border Security." *European Journal of Social Theory* 15, no. 2 (2011): 179–195.

Sánchez, Rosaura, and Beatriz Pita. *Lunar Braceros 2125–2148*. National City, CA: Calaca, 2009.

Scott, James C. *Seeing like a State: How Certain Schemes to Improve the Human Condition Have Failed*. New Haven, CT: Yale University Press, 1998.

Shaw, Ian. *Predator Empire: Drone Warfare and Full Spectrum Dominance*. Minneapolis: University of Minnesota Press, 2016.

Shellabarger, Rachel, Marcus Nils Peterson, and Erin Sills. "How Conservation and Humanitarian Groups Respond to Production of Security on the Arizona-Sonora Border." *Local Environment* 17, no. 4 (2012): 481–493.

Singer, Peter. *Animal Liberation*. New York: HarperCollins, 2002.

Sledge, Matt. "Senate Immigration Reform Proposal Backs Drones, but Critics Say They're Useless and Invasive." *HuffPost*, January 28, 2013.

Stahl, Roger. *Militainment Inc.: War, Media, and Popular Culture*. New York: Routledge, 2010.

Stumpf, Juliet. "The Crimmigration Crisis: Immigrants, Crime, and Sovereign Power." *American University Law Review* 56, no. 2 (2006): 367–420.

Tewksbury, Doug. "Crowdsourcing Homeland Security: The Texas Virtual Border-Watch and Participatory Citizenship." *Surveillance and Society* 10, nos. 3–4 (2012): 249–262.

Toffler, Alvin. *Future Shock*. New York: Bantam Books, 1970.

Trevizo, Perla. "Border Patrol Pleased with New Tech Efforts." *Arizona Daily Star*, December 27, 2015, A01.

US Customs and Border Protection. "Border Patrol Tactical Unit (BORTAC)." Accessed September 10, 2019. http://cbp.gov.

———. *CBP Strategy 2020–2025: Mission/Team/Future*. Washington, DC: US Customs and Border Protection, April 17, 2019.

———. *Concept of Operations for CBP's Predator B Unmanned Aircraft System*. Washington, DC: US Customs and Border Protection, June 29, 2010.

———. *Office of Inspector General Review 2012*. Washington, DC: US Customs and Border Protection, 2012.

———. *2012–2016 Border Patrol Strategic Plan*. Washington, DC: US Customs and Border Protection, 2012.

———. *Vision and Strategy 2020*. Washington, DC: US Customs and Border Protection, 2016.

US Department of Homeland Security. "'SBI*net* Program' Program Specific Recovery Act Plan." May 15, 2009.

———. "Secure Border Initiative." Press release, November 2, 2005. http://dhs.gov.

———. "Testimony of Michael J. Fisher, Chief, U.S. Border Patrol, U.S. Customs and Border Protection, before the House Committee on Homeland Security, Subcommittee on Border and Maritime Security: 'Does Administrative Amnesty Harm our Efforts to Gain and Maintain Operational Control of the Border?'" October 4, 2011. www.dhs.gov.

"US DHS Swamped with Proposals for Border Drones with On-Board Biometrics." *Biometric Technology Today*, June 2017. http://biometrics-today.com.

US Government Accountability Office. *Secure Border Initiative: Observations on the Importance of Applying Lessons Learned to Future Projects*. February 27, 2008.

US House of Representatives. *The Arizona Border Surveillance Technology Plan and Its Impact on Border Security: Hearing before the Subcommittee on Border and Maritime Security (Committee on Homeland Security)*. March 12, 2014.

Virilio, Paul. *The Lost Dimension*. Translated by Daniel Moshenberg. New York: Semiotext(e), 1991.

Walia, Harsha. *Undoing Border Imperialism*. Oakland, CA: AK, 2013.

Wall, Tyler, and Torin Monahan. "Surveillance and Violence from Afar: The Politics of Drones and Liminal Security-scapes." *Theoretical Criminology* 15, no. 3 (2011): 239–254.

Webb, Walter Prescott. *The Great Plains*. New York: Grosset and Dunlap, 1978.

Weber, David J. *Myth and the History of the Hispanic Southwest*. Albuquerque: University of New Mexico Press, 1988.

Weissman, Elke. *Transnational Television Drama: Special Relations and Mutual Influence between the US and the UK*. New York: Palgrave Macmillan, 2012.

Weizman, Eyal. "Introduction to the Politics of Verticality." Open Democracy, April 23, 2002. www.opendemocracy.net.

Woolley, Jane. "Border Force." Paper presented at the World Border Security Congress, Casablanca, Morocco, 2019.

Wright, Eric Olin. "Socialism and Real Utopias." In *Alternatives to Capitalism: Proposals for a Democratic Economy*, by Robin Hahnel and Erick Olin Wright, 75–105. New York: Verso, 2016.

Wright, George M., Joseph S. Dixon, and Ben H. Thompson. *Fauna of the National Parks of the United States: A Preliminary Survey of Faunal Relations in National Parks*. Washington, DC: GPO, 1933.

Wright, Will. *The Wild West: The Mythical Cowboy and Social Theory*. London: Sage, 2001.

Zureik, Elia, and Mark B. Salter. Introduction to *Global Surveillance and Policing: Borders, Security, Identity*, edited by Elia Zureik and Mark B. Salter, 1–10. Devon, UK: Willan, 2005.

INDEX

Page numbers in *italics* indicate Figures and Tables

ABOUT THE AUTHOR

CAMILLA FOJAS is Professor of Media Studies and American Studies at the University of Virginia. Her most recent books include *Zombies, Migrants, and Queers: Race and Crisis Capitalism in Pop Culture* and *Migrant Labor and Border Securities in Pop Culture.*